外国人学太极拳入门

Gateway to Taijiquan for Overseas Learners

王淑英　扈季元　主编

北京语言文化大学出版社

（京）新登字 157 号

图书在版编目（CIP）数据

外国人学太极拳入门：中英对照/王淑英、扈季元主编．
－北京：北京语言文化大学出版社，2000
ISBN 7－5619－0892－X
Ⅰ．外…
Ⅱ．①王…　②扈…
Ⅲ．太极拳－基本知识－英、汉
Ⅳ．G852.11
中国版本图书馆 CIP 数据核字（2000）第 54610 号

责任校对：顾秀丽
责任印制：乔学军
出版发行：北京语言文化大学出版社
社　　址：北京海淀区学院路 15 号　邮政编码 100083
网　　址：http：//www.blcup.com
　　　　　http：//www.blcu.edu.cn/cbs/index.htm
印　　刷：北京北林印刷厂
经　　销：全国新华书店
版　　次：2001 年 6 月第 1 版　2001 年 6 月第 1 次印刷
开　　本：787 毫米×1092 毫米　1/32　印张：6.75
字　　数：138 千字　印数：0001－2000 册
书　　号：ISBN 7－5619－0892－X/G·0078
定　　价：15.50 元

发行部电话：010－82303651　82303591
　　　传真：010－82303081
E-mail：fxb@blcu.edu.cn

前　言

太极拳是中华武术中的宝贵遗产，它是一种融防身、健体、祛病、养性于一身的健身拳术。它以其独特的运动方式及其健身价值在世界各地广泛流传而闻名于世。外国朋友通过学习具有丰富古老的中国文化内涵的太极拳运动，可以帮助他们了解中国传统的文化，促进中西文化的交融。

为满足与适应广大外国朋友学习太极拳的需求，我们从实际出发，中英文对照，图文并茂，深入浅出地以太极拳文化及技术与方法结合编写了这本教材。本书通过简单易懂的语言，为外国朋友又快又准地学习好太极拳文化及其技术提供了不可多得的学习教材，也为广大教练员指导外国朋友学习太极拳提供了必备的参考资料。

本教材编写主持人扈季元，王淑英、扈季元任主编；王伟光、那松长任副主编。翻译：周立——第一章，张志龙——第二章第一、二、三节，韦会——第二章第四节。各章节的撰稿人如下：第一章——扈季元、王伟光，第二章第一节——那松长，第二章第二节——李凤芹，第二章第三节——王淑英，第二章第四节——信立天。

本教材是对外国人进行太极拳教学的第一本教材，我们衷心希望本书对学习太极拳的外国朋友们有所帮助。

编者

Preface

Taijiquan, a health-building boxing which integrates self-defence, health-care, disease elimination and moral cultivation, is a precious legacy of Chinese martial arts. It has been well known and widely spread all over the world for its unique patterns of movement and its value of health-building. Foreign learners acquaint themselves with the rich connotation and the long history of traditional Chinese culture by practising *taijiquan* which contains its essence, thus promote the cultural communications between China and Western countries.

To meet the needs of *taijiquan* learners, we compiled this book proceeding from the practical needs—parallel Chinese and English versions, accompanied with pictures and illustrations together with simple explanations to the profound culture and techniques of *taijiquan*. It provides foreign learners with exceptional learning materials in simple language and enables them to acquire the culture and techniques of *taijiquan* quickly and correctly. Meanwhile, it also serves as a necessary reference for *taijiquan* instructors teaching foreign students.

Mr Hu Jiyuan is in charge of the compilation. Ms Wang Shuying and Mr Hu Jiyuan are the chief editors and Ms Wang Weiguang and Mr Na Songchang are the associate chief editors. It is translated by Zhou Li (Chapter One), Zhang Zhilong (Sections

One, Two and Three of Chapter Two), Wei Hui (Section Four of Chapter Two).

The writers are as follows:

Chapter One: Hu Jiyuan and Wang Weiguang

Chapter Two: Section One — Na Songchang

Section Two — Li Fengqin

Section Three — Wang Shuying

Section Four — Xin Litian

This is the first textbook ever published in China on the subject intended for overseas readers. We hope the readers will find the book helpful in their learning of *taijiquan*.

Editors

目　　录

Contents

第一章　太极拳运动的基本知识

Chapter One: Essentials of Taijiquan

一、太极拳的起源与发展

太极拳是中华武术的重要拳种之一。它取历代名家拳法之所长,结合古代导引、吐纳之术,运用阴阳学说以及中医理论的经络学说创编而成。

太极拳因其动作如行云流水连绵不断,用太极阴阳之哲理来解释拳义而得名。它内容丰富,既能技击防身,又可修身养性,具有很高的锻炼价值和医疗保健作用。

据武术史学家考证,太极拳最早出现于清初河南温县陈家沟。在近300多年的发展过程中,经过无数太极高手的不断改进和创新,演变形成了陈、杨、吴、武、孙式等各种具有不同风格、特点的流派。

各流派的太极拳都有自己的练拳套路,陈式老架有五路,近代流传陈式太极拳有一路83式,二路71式。陈式新架套路也有两种:一种是“小圈拳”,另一种是“赵堡架”。杨式太极拳有85式。吴式太极拳有老架83式及经过简化的37式。当今社会流传广泛的是24式简化太极拳、32式简化太极拳和48式太极拳。

24式简化太极拳是在杨式太极拳的基础上,根据由简入繁、循序渐进、易学易练的原则改编而成的普及套路,并配以旋律优美的民族音乐。在1990年第11届亚运会开幕式的团体表演,赢得了极大的轰动。

I. The Origin and Evolution of *Taijiquan*

Taijiquan, one of the most important boxings in Chinese *wushu*, was established upon the basis of Taoist breathing exercises①, applying the theory of *yin* and *yang*② and the theory of *jingluo*③ in traditional Chinese medicine.

The essence of *taijiquan* lies in the diagram of cosmological scheme. *Taijiquan* is famous for its smooth movements and *yin* and *yang* as its philosophical essence. With rich contents, it is designed not only to attack and defend, but also to cultivate oneself. Therefore, it is a highly-valued, health-care exercise.

Based on the historical study by *wushu* historians, *taijiquan* made its debut in Wenxian County, Henan Province in early Qing Dynasty. During its over 300 years of development, it has been improved and enriched by a number of masters. Among different *taijiquan* schools are the Chen style, the Yang style, the Wu style, Wu Yuxiang style and the Sun style, which are different styles each with their own distinct characteristics.

Every *taijiquan* school sets its own package of skills and steps. The Chen-style *taijiquan* falls into two types——the old and the new frames. The old frame has five sets. Two sets are seen in modern Chen-style *taijiquan*. One set with 83 forms, the other 71 forms. The new

---

① Taoist breathing exercises: a Taoist art to achieve longevity by breathing fresh air in and the useless air out.

② the theory of yin and yang: In Chinese philosophy and medicine, *yin* and *yang* are the two opposing principles in nature, the former feminine and negative, the latter masculine and positive.

③ jingluo: main and collateral channels, passages in the human body through which vital energy circulates and along which the acupuncture points are distributed.

太极拳和其他拳种相比，具有柔和性、完整性、连贯性、圆活性等鲜明的拳法特点。

(1) 柔和性　太极拳架式平稳舒展，动作轻缓柔和，紧而不僵，松而不懈，柔中寓刚，刚柔相济。

(2) 完整性　太极拳要求全身一动无不动，一静无不静，动作上下相随，气意内外相合，全身各部位紧密配合，完整一体。

(3) 连贯性　太极拳套路从始而终，首尾相接，虚实变化，姿势转换，互相衔接，一气贯穿。

(4) 圆活性　太极拳要求立身中正、左右转换，所有动作均走圆形曲线，包括大、小、平、立、椭圆等。

近年来，随着中外文化交流日益扩大，太极拳作为中外文化交流的友好使者，走向了世界。许多外国人都喜欢上太极拳这项中华传统武术项目，他们中间的许多人来到中国学习太极拳，并把太极精神带回自己的祖国。愿太极拳这朵中华武林的奇葩绽放在世界之苑。

frame Chen-style *taijiquan* includes "Small Circle Boxing" and "Zhaobao Frame". The Yang-style *taijiquan* comprises 85 moves, while the Wu-style includes the old frame of 83 moves and the simplified form of 37 moves. At present the 24-move, the 32-move and the 48-move simplified *taijiquan* have gained great popularity across the country.

The 24-move simplified *taijiquan* is developed from the Yang style under the principle of being easy to learn and practise, and from simple to complex. Its charm is in part attributable to its beautiful background Chinese folk music. In the opening ceremony of the 11th Asian Games, it was shown as a group performances, which caused a great sensation in the spectators' circle.

Taijiquan is characterized by features like: softness, wholeness, continuity, circular movements.

(1) Softness: The stances of *taijiquan* are steady and stretchy. The movements are slow and soft, tightened but not clumsy, relaxed but not slack, which is a good example of tempering force with softness.

(2) Wholeness: *Taijiquan* requires wholeness in actions, in other words, different parts of the body move or stop in harmony and coordination. There is an association of activity and stillness.

(3) Continuity: All the stances of *taijiquan* are performed consistently from start to end with a smooth shift between every two postures. It is known to be a continuum of force and movements, which should be practised at a stretch.

(4) Circular movements: All the movements take such shapes as a circle, a curve or an oval. A firm standing and good coordination between the left and the right is necessary.

Nowadays, with a broader cultural communication, *taijiquan* has carried with itself good wishes wherever it goes in the world. A lot of foreigners are fascinated by this charming Chinese sport. They come to China to learn *taijiquan* and take home *taiji* spirits. May *taijiquan* forever flourish and shine in martial arts home and abroad.

二、太极拳与中国文化

太极拳是在中国传统文化的影响下成形和发展的。学习和了解太极拳形成与发展的文化背景,将有助于外国人理解太极拳拳理,为学好太极拳技术打下基础。

1. 太极拳与中国传统哲学密切相关

太极拳得名于《周易·系辞》的"易有太极,是生两仪",它直接参照太极图形编排动作,而形成自己独特的运动形式。所谓"太极",在中国哲学中指派生万物的本源,包含动、静,阴、阳两个方面,具有动而生阳,静而生阴,既对立又统一,相互消长、转化,不断运动、变化的特性。从太极拳要求柔缓浑圆,强调"以静制动"上看,它与老子"重柔主静"的思想相通。从太极拳的动作要求上看,那种精、气、神的和谐统一,一动俱动、一到俱到的"内外合一"的整体运动规范,是受中国传统的"天人合一"观念的影响的结果。太极拳的动作路线和规格要求多表现为欲左先右、欲开先合、欲伸先屈、欲紧先松等反向着手开始动作的表现形式,可溯源《老子》的"将欲歙之,必固张之;将欲弱之,必固强之;将欲废之,必固兴之;将欲取之,必固与之"的辩证思想。

由此可见,中国传统的哲学思想对太极拳理论及其技术的形成有着至关重要的影响。同时,我们应看到,由于中国传统的哲学流派如儒、道、理等学说都注重养生,这样,太极拳在受到传统哲学影响的同时,必然会与中国传统养生文化和医学发生一种天然的姻缘关系,如

Ⅱ. *Taijiquan* and the Chinese Culture

Taijiquan originated and developed under the influence of traditional Chinese culture. An understanding of its cultural background will assure a better understanding of the morality of *taijiquan* and will hence lay a solid foundation for the learning.

1. *Taijiquan* Is Closely Tied to Traditional Chinese Philosophy

Taijiquan won its name from *The Book of Changes of the Zhou Dynasty*. As the book puts it, "Where there is *taiji*, there is peace and harmony between the positive and the negative." Its unique form originated from the diagram of cosmological scheme. In Chinese philosophy, *taiji* refers to the ultimate source of the universe. It contains two opposite aspects of activity and inertia, with the former bearing *yang* and the latter *yin*. *Yang* and *yin* are contradictory yet complementary. There is an increase in *yang* if one moves and an increase in *yin* if one remains still. *Taijiquan*, by highlighting "Softness can counter hardness", complies with Laozi's idea of softness and motionlessness. The conception of absoluteness, coherence and unbrokenness in movements, and the unity of spirit, energy and concentration exemplified in *taijiquan* draw its inspiration from the theory that "Man is an integral part of nature." The route and movements of *taijiquan* largely embody in "Go right first when you intend to go left; bend first when you intend to stretch; tighten first when you intend to let loose." The traceable source is rooted in the dialectical idea of Laozi— "Open in order to close; weaken in order to strengthen; abolish in order to establish; give in order to take."

阴阳平衡论、精、气、神等等学说，对太极拳理论的逐步完善起到了重要的指导作用。因此，了解中国传统养生（医学）文化对太极拳的发展的影响，会使我们进一步了解使其赖以生成与发展的文化背景的全貌。

2. 太极拳与中国养生文化

太极拳运动之所以在中国经久不衰，是因为其独特的健身、祛病、养生、自卫等深受广大人民喜爱的功效，而这一点又得益于中国传统养生（医学）文化。受其影响的太极拳拳理及其功法使中国传统养生文化在健身应用上变成现实。因此，了解养生文化对太极拳运动的影响，将有助于外国人理解太极拳文化。

(1) 阴阳学说论

中国古代阴阳学说最早发源于公元前八世纪的西周末年。到了战国末至西汉初期的《易经》中，阴阳学说才在哲学领域中得到较全面系统的发挥，《周易·系辞》中称："刚柔相推而生变化"；"日月相推而明生焉"；"寒暑相推而岁成焉。"可见，世界的万事万物无不在阴阳相互作用中变化、生长。在此基础上《易经》提出的"一阴一阳之谓道"的对立统一的辩证思路，被视为万事万物运动变化的总规律。如后世科学家基本上是遵循了《易经》的辩证思想，用对立统一的规律来解释人体生命活动现象的。明代医学家张介宾在《类经·阴阳类》中曾指出："道者阴阳之理也。阴阳者，一分为二也。太极动而生阳，静而生阴，天生于动，地生于静，故阴阳为天地之

Hence we can see that the traditional ideas of Chinese philosophy play an important role in the theorization and formation of the skills of *taijiquan*. It follows that, since separate schools of Chinese philosophy such as Confucianism, Taoism and Neo-Confucianism of the Song and Ming Dynasties all attach great importance to nourishing life, *taijiquan* is bound to have genealogy with the tradition and medical science of health-care, e.g. the balance theory between *yin* and *yang*, the theory of spirit, energy and concentration ,etc. all function to consummate the theory of *taijiquan*. The mentioning of the tradition of health-care enables us to be further aware of its evolution.

2. *Taijiquan* and the Chinese Health-Care Tradition

Taijiquan has flourished with its functions of disease-curing, health-keeping and self-defence. All of them are clearly attributable to the impact of traditional health-preserving culture which turns theory into reality. So, an understanding of the influence of the culture of health-preserving on *taijiquan* will help us understand the culture in *taijiquan* better.

(1) The theory of *yin* and *yang*

The theory of *yin* and *yang* turned up in 800 B.C. It didn't contribute its due share to philosophy until the end of the period of the Warring States. *The Book of Changes* said, "Change comes from the applied force between softness and hardness; light comes from the applied force between the sun and the moon; season comes from the transition between hotness and coldness." It is thus evident that everything of nature grows and changes under the force of *yin* and *yang*. "*Yin* and *yang* reflects Tao" had symbolically represented all changes in the cosmos. Scientists of later generations inherited this philosophy to expound human life and activities. Zhang Jiebin, a medical scientist of the Ming

道。”这说明了中国传统医学理论将阴阳的相互消长作用视为人体生命活动的根本。换言之，自然界都是阴阳二者相互作用的产物。太极拳正是依据前人的阴阳学说的根本原理，创编了独特的拳理、结构和特征。从太极拳传统套路的动作和结构上看，都是由两个相互对立、相互依存、相互制约并转化而又统一的阴阳物质所组成。拳理中的静与动、柔与刚、虚与实、浑圆与松沉的要求无不体现阴阳物质的相互间关系。如传统套路中的手挥琵琶、掤捋挤按等动作将阴阳合为一体，相互对立又依存的一招一势的阴阳运转极佳地展现了阴阳学说理论在太极拳式中的具体运用。

(2) 精、气、神的和谐统一

精、气、神在中国传统养生理论中占有重要的位置，被视为人体生命活动的三个基本要素。它与阴阳、五行学说理论一样与中国古代哲学存在千丝万缕的联系，认为世间一切物质现象都是精、气、神的存在形式。如老、庄子认为“道是万物源，而气则是道的另一种表达方式，万物都是由气化生的。”《庄子知北游》称：“人之生，气之聚也，聚则生，散则死……故曰通天下一气耳。”把气看成了构成万物的基本要素。又如中华医学理论认为，“精”是人体生命活动的重要物质，它是由先天的肾精和后天饮食水谷的精气所结合的化生物质。“气”是维持生理功能的，“气”的存在是通过一定的生理功能表现出来的，它的生成又与肾、脾、胃、肺等脏腑器官密切相关。由此可见，“精”和“气”是人体生命活动的重要物质基础。

Dynasty pointed out in his *Book of Categories*, "*Yin* and *yang* is Tao. They are two opposite sides. According to *taiji*, *yang* grows in mobility and *yin* grows in immobility." It proved that Chinese traditional medical science took the two complementary interactive forces as the base of human activity. In other words, even nature is the product of the interaction between *yin* and *yang*. Its theorization, composition and characteristics are all created on this basis. As far as movements and composition are concerned, both of them are linked to *yin* and *yang* that are opposite, interdependent and mutually restricting. The interaction between *yang* and *yin* can be seen everywhere — in activity and inertia, in hardness and softness, in excess and deficiency. For instance, opposite yet interdependent moves as in "Playing the Lute" in the traditional routine of *taijiquan*, integrating *yin* and *yang* , echoes the application of the *yin* and *yang* theory in *taijiquan*.

(2) *The unity of spirit, energy and concentration*

Spirit, energy and concentration, three essentials of life, are highly valued in Chinese health-care culture. Like the *yin* and *yang* theory and the five-element theory①, it is directly associated with ancient Chinese philosophy, holding that all material phenomena take the form of spirit, energy and concentration. According to Laozi and Zhuangzi *tao* is the source of nature and energy is an alternate representation of *tao*. Zhuangzi claims in his book, "Life is an accumulation of energy. Accumulation of energy leads to life, while dispersal of energy leads to

---

① The five elements (metal, wood, water, fire and earth) were believed by the ancients to compose the physical universe and the five-element theory was later used in traditional Chinese medicine to explain various physiological and pathological phenomena.

太极拳所要求的内外兼修、注重一开一合的调吸运动的着眼点正是来源于养生理论的“养气”、“补气”的要求。

“神”的生成以先天之“精”为基础，以后天的精气补养而成，它是人体生命活动表象的称谓，包括意识思维活动，脏腑、经络、气血等机体活动效能和外在的表现。正如《黄帝内经》所称：“故生之来谓之精，两精相搏谓之神”。说明了“气”产生于“精”，“精”的生化有赖于“气”，而“精气”的共同作用表现为“神”。人体生命活动的正常运转都依赖“神”的维持，传统医学视“神”为人体生命活动的主宰，正如《黄帝内经》所提到的“得神者昌，失神者死”的论断。在传统养生文化的影响下，传统太极拳练习方法分内功与外功，俗称内练精、气、神，外练筋、骨、皮，就是这个道理。练习太极拳，通过调心、调吸、调身等动作，提高了脏腑、消化吸收和气化功能，促使“精”足、“气”充、“神”旺，达到强身健体。这种形神兼养、养神为先的锻炼方法，鲜明地代表了民族特色。

除了阴阳学说，精、气、神相互依附、促进的论点对太极拳的生成演变产生过巨大影响之外，还有传统哲学的五行学说、天人相应观念和古代经络学说等，都对太极拳的创编与发展产生过较深的影响，由于篇幅原因本文不再论述。

death." Chinese medical theory believes that spirit, as a vital matter of life, consists of inborn kidney essence and the essence contained in food and drink we consume everyday. The existence of energy is manifested by certain physiological functions, and its formation is closely connected with the internal organs such as the kidneys, lungs, spleen and stomach. That is why we say spirit and energy is the bottom line to interpret *taijiquan*. *Taijiquan* calls for cultivation from both inside and outside, its breathing exercises meeting the demand of supplying and nourishing energy.

Concentration comes from inborn essence and acquired energy. It is a denotation of life representations including the activities of the brain, the internal organs, the *jingluo* and the blood. Just as it is argued in *The Yellow Emperor's Book on Internal Activities*, "Spirit is inborn, and concentration is the effect of spirit." That is to say, energy comes from spirit, the change of spirit is reliant on energy, and the effect of spirit and energy is expressed in concentration upon which regular human activities depend. Traditional Chinese medical science views concentration as dominant in human life. Under the influence of health-care culture, the approach to *taijiquan* practice goes in two branches: the exercises to benefit the internal organs as well as the exercises to benefit the muscles and bones. Regulation of the brain, the breath and the body enhances a person's digesting and assimilating ability to achieve luxuriant spirit, sufficient energy and exuberant concentration. To build up one's body by giving concentration practice priority sharply defines its national feature.

Beside the theory of *yin* and *yang*, the unity of spirit, energy and concentration, other philosophical ideas such as the five-element theory, the *jingluo* theory mentioned above and the concept that "Men act in harmony with nature", etc., all occupy their respective places in the formation and maturation of *taijiquan*.

三、太极拳与西方体育运动的文化比较

1. 文化上的差异

作为传统的人体运动方式的太极拳和西方体育运动的项目一样，其方式都是指向人体自身的，都是在强壮体魄这一客观效能下完成各自目的的，这点表现出人类的共性。但由于太极拳运动受几千年古老文化的影响和规范，必然与受西方文化影响的现代体育项目大相径庭，两种文化所产生的运动方式和思路必然产生碰撞，而这种文化上的碰撞又是外国人学习和理解太极拳文化的难点，解除这一难点，我们就必须对各自赖以生成的文化背景加以梳理和比较。

太极拳运动成型于明清时期，它强调的是阴阳组合的生命律动，外取神态，内表心灵，受到中国传统文化精神的“天人合一”、“阴阳之道”所支配，其身体运动观不是积极地引向外在的显示，而是导向内心的自审。这种“天人合一”，“内外兼修”，追求“有意无意”之真意的无极境界的运动与西方体育现象迥然相异。

西方体育运动的主流来自于古希腊的奥林匹克运动，从运动形式、规则到竞赛方式等都脱胎于古奥运会的竞技，包括近代工业文明以后才诞生的不少运动项目，其设计思路仍然具有沉厚的西方文化特征。如西方传统的篮球和拳击运动，强调“主动攻击”、“表现自我”等意识，

Ⅲ. A Comparison between the Cultural Background of *Taijiquan* and That of Western Sports

1. Cultural Disparity

As a traditional sport, *taijiquan* was the same as Western sports, targeting upon oneself and achieving his own goals by building up the body, which is a general character of human beings. But a wide gap exists between the two different practices, because both of them are the products of their own traditions. Cultural conflicts make *taijiquan* a hot potato for foreigners. To get the obstacle out of the way, we must aim at a thorough understanding of the different cultural backgrounds where they evolved and grew.

Taijiquan debutted during the Ming and Qing Dynasties. It emphasizes a combination of *yin* and *yang*, and inner activities and outer actions, which clearly projects the spirit of traditional Chinese culture —"Human is part of nature." The outlook of the practice is not supposed to be extroverted, but to be introverted. A conscious or unconscious pursuit of the consummation is where *taijiquan* sets its ultimate target, which goes along quite another track from any Western sport items.

The mainstream of Western sports originated from the Olympic Games in ancient Greece. From their form of movements to the rules and ways of the competition, Western sports were all born out of the athletics of ancient Olympics. Even in some sport items that emerged after the Industrial Revolution, the thinking still represents the features of the Western culture. Take basketball and boxing for example. These two sports items lay stress on the ideas of offence and self-show, and pay

重技术体系的构建，极佳表现了“具体”、“对立”、“推理”等西方传统的思维方式。由此可见，由于文化背景不同，思维方式不同，太极拳运动与西方体育相互交融时不可避免地出现文化上的差异。

2. 太极拳运动和西方体育运动的文化比较

两种不同的传统文化，直接影响各自传统体育项目的不同特色，反映出各自体育背景的文化源泉。从西方体育运动项目上看，就其源泉而言，与宗教、游戏、军事和劳动的关系密切。它在西方哲学的具体分析、对立、推理等原则的影响下得到发展，它的运动观则注重外在的、个人的、权利的、对立的和有观赏性的表象。如拳击运动，以一种个体的人格精神的展现为目的的活动，表现出主动出击、直来直去、展现自我的争斗形式。又如，典型的西方篮球运动具有鲜明的目的性，善于具体技术、战术分析和严谨的训练程序，不能不说是西方传统思维方式和文化的又一体现。可以讲，西方现代体育作为一种具体文化形态和它的背景文化有着明显的同构。

然而，太极拳运动与西方体育运动比较，面貌就迥异了。它不需要直接对抗来表现自我，主要通过个体的演练达到修身养性和强壮自我。这种身心俱练、动静结合、含蓄待发、具有丰富内涵的独特方式，显示出中国传统体育通过锻炼身体来以外达内、由表及里、有形的身体活动促成无形的精神升华、实现理想人格的塑造。与西方体育价值观形成鲜明的反差。这种反差的成因，来

great attention to the systemization of skills, which is a clear reflection of the traditional Western thinking of "concreteness", "opposition" and "reasoning". Due to the cultural disparity and different thinking models, difficulties occur in blending *taijiquan* — something typically Chinese — with Western sports.

2. A Cultural Comparison between *Taijiquan* and Western Sports

Two separate cultures feature their own sports. Western sports, closely tied to religion, games, labor and military affairs, have developed under the influence of Western philosophical principles — concrete analysis, antagonism and inference. Their rules are concerned with manifestations of externalism, individuality, rights, antagonism and appreciation. Boxing, designed to demonstrate individuality, has a fighting layout which is offensive, straight and self expressive. The game of basketball with clearly defined goals is well-known for its skill analysis, tactic analysis and strict training courses. It is another reflection of Western culture and thinking model. So we can draw a bold conclusion that Western sports, a specific cultural activity, has the same configuration as their cultural background.

Taijiquan is very much different from Western sports. It does not have to display itself through direct opposition. The target of self-cultivation and health-care is achieved through individual exercise. It is a culturally-saturated exercise which aims to discipline both the mind and the body, and promote intangible spiritual distillation through tangible body movements to realize ideal characterization. The striking contrast between *taijiquan* and Western sports results from the different cultural backgrounds. *Taijiquan* is based upon the theory of *yin* and *yang*.

源于各自背景文化的影响。我们知道，太极拳运动是以中国的阴阳学说为理论基础。它集中国拳术、传统哲学、传统医学、养生文化为一身，才成为中国传统的体育代表性项目。这种文化的根，使太极拳具备了民族的风格。因此，只有了解其背景文化才能理解太极拳运动的内涵，并达到“精”、“气”、“神”的协调统一。否则，就会出现在同一项目中表现出不同风格的运动景象。如外国运动员在表演太极拳时，从拳式到动作、套路和技术上应该说掌握的比较正确。但我们总是感觉他们缺点什么，与中国运动员相比总有着差异，这种差别不在服饰上，更不在相貌上和肤色上，差别就在于气质上。这就是文化的根，它反映出了一种文化不同于另一种文化的独特性。因此，外国人学习太极拳，首先应了解其根，理解其文化内涵，才能把集“武功、养生和艺术性”的太极拳技术真正学到手。

差异较大的中西方体育运动项目的确能启发我们站在宏观的文化立场上看问题。实践证明，通过两种文化的相互交融、学习，完全可以消除学习上的难点。同时也应看到，从中西方体育文化的特点上讲，并无优劣之分，只是在各自的背景文化影响下，表现出个性不同而已。我们有了这方面的认识，就能不断地提高对太极拳文化的认知水平，克服难点，走向趋同。

四、太极拳的健身作用

太极拳运动是集中国武术、传统医学、经络学说、养生学为一身的内外兼修、动静结合、老少皆宜的一种独

Nourished by Chinese boxings, health-care culture, Chinese traditional philosophy and Chinese medical science, *taijiquan* is an symbolic knockout of traditional Chinese sports. The soil where it is rooted provides a cultural identity for it. Therefore, to understand the connotation of *taijiquan* and to achieve the harmony of spirit, energy and mind, one must go back to Chinese culture. Otherwise misinterpretation will result in inharmonious practices of the sport. Foreigners performing *taijiquan* are liable to master forms, expertise and movements at the expense of its essence. Compared with Chinese players, foreign learners mark themselves not in dressing, nor in appearance or in complexion, but in disposition. Therefore, it is essential for foreigners to have an understanding of Chinese culture before they can assure a perfect mastery of *taijiquan* as an entity of health preserving, martial arts and artistic value.

From a cultural perspective, hurdles in the way can surely be cleared away through a broad cultural contact, which gives an accurate account of *taijiquan* and Western sports as cultural fruits. Of course, we are not to judge which is favorable and which is unfavorable, but frame our cultural recognition of the individualistic marks of Chinese and Western sports.

Ⅳ. *Taijiquan* as a Sport to Keep Fit

Taijiquan is a unique body-building exercise for the young and the aged alike. It is a popular sport beneficial to the internal organs as well as the skin and bones.

特的健身运动。它通过自身的内审和刚柔相济的动作调整身体内部的功能,达到增强体质、抵抗疾病、祛病强身的目的。它的内练精、气、神,外练筋骨皮的功法特点,深受人们喜爱。下面简要介绍太极拳对人体的健身作用。

1. 太极拳运动对中枢神经系统的作用

中枢神经系统的功能是调节人体各系统正常活动,形成一个对立统一的整合体,使人体内外环境达到相对平衡。神经系统失去平衡必然影响各系统的均衡活动,引起疾病。因此,养护好中枢神经系统是至关重要的。而太极拳运动是养护神经系统的首选项目,它在人的意识主导下进行锻炼,进入意守丹田、排除杂念的境界,使大脑皮层得到了积极的休息(抑制),通过积极的保护,可使大脑皮层由于过度的兴奋所导致的机能紊乱加以纠正和调节,达到养护作用。

2. 太极拳运动对内脏器官的作用

太极拳练功时的轻、松、柔、慢、均、细、长、深的调息方式,对提高人的精、气、神的作用有显著的影响。

体内各器官的相互协调与均衡是身体强健的首要条件,如某一器官出现失调,就会影响其他器官的平衡,疾病也就产生了。因此,它们是相互关联、缺一不可的有机整体。所以养护内脏器官的协调和均衡能力,是人们健康生存所必需的。

结合太极拳以丹田为轴心的内在气脉运动,从均匀又深长的调息配合胸腹不断开合的运动的特点上看,这种运动方式正是人们养护内脏器官的极佳手段。实践

1. Its Positive Effect on the Central Nervous System

The leading function of the central nervous system is to regulate the activities of the systems of a human body, so that the body can balance its internal and external environment. If this function of the central nervous system is upset, diseases are likely to result. Therefore, it is important to maintain one's central nervous system and *taijiquan* is such a working option. *Taijiquan* is practised under the direction of consciousness, concentrating on *dantian*, dispersing distracting thoughts and relaxing the cerebral cortex so that overexcitement-induced disorder is put right.

2. Its Postive Effect on the Internal Organs

The breathing exercise of *taijiquan* is regulated in a soft, loose, slow, even, long and deep manner, which will sharpen concentration and restore spirit and energy.

The coordination and balance of the internal organs are of vital importance to body-building. Organs of a human body work integratedly and interdependently in an unbroken chain. If one link ceases to be effective, diseases will break into it.

With *dantian* as an axis around which the energy circulates, *taijiquan* is characterized by even and deep breathing in accompany with the opening and closing of the chest and abdomen, which is the best access to the maintenance of the internal organs. It is proved that the breathing exercises of *taijiquan* can speed up the movements of the diaphragm three to four times. It results in the increase of the abdominal pressure, thus all the internal organs can enjoy gentle and even massage, the flexibility of the organs and the balance between them are preserved, and the improvements of the breathing, metabolic, digesting and recycle systems build one's immunity to keep one away from diseases.

证明,太极拳的调息运动促进了体内横膈肌的上下移动,活动幅度比平常增加三到四倍,活动幅度的增强改变了腹腔内压,使各个器官受到了柔和均匀的挤压和按摩,增强了器官的柔韧性和蠕动性,并达到相互间的平衡协调性,从而使体内的呼吸、代谢、消化、循环等系统产生一系列的良性变化,提高了自身的免疫功能,达到了自治、自愈、自强的目的。

3. 太极拳运动对人体的骨骼、肌肉功能的作用

太极拳运动的动作规格和浑圆运作方式对人体的骨骼和肌肉的协调刺激作用较为明显。从“外柔内刚、刚柔相济、松紧协调一致”的动作要求上看,它既符合“阴阳之理”,又与人体运动生物力学规律相一致,它以人体内外中枢(中丹田、腰)进行一动俱动、含蓄待发的全身内外整体圆形的运动表现,使身体活动部位全面,动作幅度可大可小,改善了全身各关节、肌肉周围软组织的血液循环,疏通了经络,强健了肌肉,骨骼,从而预防了骨质疏松和骨刺的形成。特别对中老年人的腰肌劳损、颈椎病、肩周炎、骨质增生病症的预防和治疗有显著的功效。

4. 太极拳运动对循环系统的作用

人体循环系统具有为人体正常生命活动供能从而保证人体新陈代谢的功能。养护好循环系统对延缓人体机能衰老、提高人体活力具有积极的意义。

太极拳的内外柔缓的螺旋式运作方式使人体各系统

3. Its Positive Effect on the Muscles and Bones

The curve-like movements of *taijiquan* strongly stimulate the muscles and bones. The demand of *taijiquan* movements—"couple hardness with softness"—accords with the theory of *yin* and *yang* as well as with the laws of biomechanics. The circular movements puts the body in a kind of touch-and-go status, especially the mid-*dantian* and waist. The scope of movements is flexible and all parts of the body are exercised. In this way, the blood circulation of all the joints and tissues around the muscles is accelerated. By dredging the channels inside the body and strengthening the muscles and bones, bony spur and osteoporosis can be prevented. Besides, *taijiquan* is particularly helpful to the prevention and curing of lumbar muscle degeneration, cervical spondylopathy, scapulohumeral periarthritis and hyperosteogeny, which often occur to the seniors.

4. Its Positive Effect on the Circulatory System

The circulatory system provides all the energy needed for human activity and thereby insures metabolism. Nourishing and protecting the circulatory system can postpone senility and enhance vigour.

As it is mentioned above, the spiral movings in *taijiquan* massage the internal organs. Furthermore, they also do good to the arteries, veins and capillaries. By exercising *taijiquan*, the elasticity of the vessels is improved, blood viscosity is reduced, blood flow rate is accelerated and vasodilation is achieved. More blood runs to the brain and heart to perform a better metabolism. A vigorous unity of spirit, energy and concentration promises longevity.

受到轻柔挤压、按摩,从内脏到四肢、从动静脉管到远端的毛细血管都得到了锻炼,改善和提高了大小血管的弹性和力量,达到了降低血液粘稠度、加快血流速度、舒张周身血管、增加心脑血流量的目的,从而提高了新陈代谢的质量,促进了精血的保养和气血的舒畅,从根本上保证了人体“精”、“气”、“神”的旺盛,最终实现延年益寿的目的。

5. 太极拳运动对人体五官功能的作用

人体五官是反映人的精神风貌的直接窗口,俗话讲“眼睛是心灵的窗口”,就是这个道理。所以保养好五官功能是十分重要的。

太极拳运动对人体的头、眼、鼻、舌、耳、面的松正、自然、聚精敛意的要求,有益于疏通五官各部位的神经,使肌肉松正,协调运作,自然、松正的运作使得五官血液充盈,充盈的血液不断地扩张周边毛细血管,滋养着五官各部位,从而保持了正常的功能。通过练习太极拳,人的眼神变得明亮,面部红润,就证明了练太极拳具有明目、滋养皮肤之功效。

6. 太极拳运动对培养人的性格的作用

良好的性格和道德修养是心理健康的重要标志。太极拳运动除了具有强身健体之功效外,还具有培养人积极进取、调畅神志和情绪之作用。

太极拳动作要求人们“精神内守”的目的就是要培养练习者用神专一、内心宁静、动中取静的境界,以达到

5. Its Positive Effect on the Five Sense Organs

The five sense organs mirror the spiritual outlook. As the saying goes, "The eyes are the windows of the soul." Therefore, it is essential to assure the functions of the five sense organs.

Taijiquan requires a relaxed, concentrated and upright state of the eyes, ears, lips, nose and tongue to dredge the facial nerves. The constant dilation of the capillaries makes them resilient and better nourish the five sense organs to maintain their functions. Bright eyes and ruddy face appear after one practises *taijiquan* for a period of time, which proves that *taijiquan* can nourish the eyes as well as the skin.

6. Its Positive Effect on One's Disposition

A good disposition and self-cultivation is the symbol of a wholesome soul. Beside its effect to body-building, *taijiquan* also helps one to control his temper and encourages one to keep forging ahead.

Taijiquan calls for withdrawal of the spirit to attain concentration, calmness and combination of mobility and immobility. It balances the internal environment to apply one's mind to objective principles. "Peace coexists with an ease mind; restlessness coexists with a confused mind. Peace can cover restlessness." This is the opinion ancient Chinese people held to cultivate their inborn nature. *Taijiquan* makes people resistant to outside temptations. It is generally acknowledged that *taijiquan* practitioners can get rid of depressions while maintaining a good mood. So practising *taijiquan* is the best way to help one to be good-mannered.

“修性以保神，安心以全身”，使体内环境协调平和，使心理处于一种适当的中和状态，以求符合事物正常运行的客观规律。正如古人所云“心安则静，心乱则躁，以静制躁”的养性之理，太极拳“动中取静”的功法能提高人的抵抗外界诱惑的能力已被人们所共识，它的自如排除忧闷、舒畅情绪、积极进取的功效，是培养人们真正达到不求静而静的良好性格及道德修养境界的最佳锻炼手段。太极拳运动深受人们的喜爱，道理就在其中。

五、怎样学练太极拳

首先，不要怕难。因为太极拳的每一个动作几乎都是全身各个部位同时活动，且多数动作走弧形、环形或旋形，并要求上下相随，初学者往往顾此失彼，难以全部做到。同时太极拳要求两腿虚实分明，绝大部分时间都是一条腿弯立着负担全部体重，做起来很费劲。因此有些人学不几天就畏缩了，不学了。其实，只要不怕困难，学习方法得当，先打好基础，闯过开头这一关，以后学习就比较容易了。

其次，要采取循序渐进的学习方法。

1. 开好头，练好基本功

根据太极拳所需要的身体能力，初学者主要应学练“太极桩功”中的平行步、弓步、虚步站和“柔韧基本功”，以增强腿部力量和肩、腰、髋等关节周围肌肉、韧带的

Ⅴ. How to Learn and Practise *Taijiquan*

First of all, one must not be afraid of difficulties. Since every movement of *taijiquan* involves simultaneous moving of almost all parts of the body, which follow either a curve, a circle or a spine, beginners often attend to one thing and lose sight of another. Meanwhile, *taijiquan* requires either an empty step or a solid step. In other words, only one leg undertakes the weight of the body most of the time. This makes the practice hard and some people give up after practising it for a few days. In fact, so long as one has perseverance and learn step by step, a foundation can be laid to make further study much easier.

1. A Good Beginning Is Half Done——Practise the Basic Skills

In terms of physical strength, beginners should practise parallel step, bow step and empty step in *taijiquan* stake exercises together with pliability exercises to strengthen their legs and to enhance pliability of the muscles and ligaments around the shoulders, waist and hips, which will lay a good foundation for successful practice.

(1) Pliability exercises

Pliability is one of the basic skills of martial arts, concerning the arms, waist and legs.

柔韧性,为学练太极拳打下腿部静力性力量和身体主要关节运动幅度的基础。

(1) 柔韧性基本功

“柔韧性基本功”是武术基本功法之一。主要包括“臂功”、“腰功”、“腿功”三类。其主要作用是使初学者具备习武的柔韧素质和体现动作幅度的能力。

a. 臂功:主要有压肩、抱臂等。其作用主要是伸拉肩关节周围的肌肉和韧带,增加以肩关节为轴的上肢运动幅度。

b. 腰动:主要“俯腰”、“涮腰”等,其作用主要是伸拉该关节周围的肌肉和韧带,增加腰髋关节的运动幅度和灵活性。

c. 腿动:一种是压腿,主要有正压腿、弓步压腿、仆步压腿等。其作用主要是慢速伸拉髋关节和大腿前、后及内侧的肌群和韧带,增加以髋关节为轴的下肢运动幅度。另一种是踢腿,主要有正踢腿、侧踢腿、外摆腿(由前到侧踢)、里合腿(由侧到前踢)。其作用主要是快速伸拉髋关节和大腿前、后及内侧的肌肉韧带,增加以髋关节为轴的下肢的运动幅度和力量。

(2) 太极桩功

“太极桩功”对太极拳的初学者主要有以下三个方面的作用:第一,使初学者做好学练太极的心理准备。“心静体松,专心致志”是学好太极拳和取得太极拳锻炼效果的首要心理条件。在学练太极拳之前先练“太极桩功”,可以在克服腿部肌肉酸疼的过程中,使初学者做好

a. Exercises of the arms

This includes pressing the shoulders and swinging the arms, etc. The purpose is to stretch the muscles and ligaments of the shoulders and activate the arms.

b. Exercises of the waist

This includes bending and turning the waist. The purpose is to stretch the muscles and ligaments and to obtain more active and flexible moves of the waist and the hips.

c. Exercises of the legs

This includes pressing the legs and kicking. Pressing the legs consists of forward press, bow press and side press, and kicking consists of forward kick, side kick and lotus kick. The difference between pressing and kicking is that the former stretches the muscles and ligaments slowly, while the latter do it much faster.

(2) *Taijiquan* stake exercises

For beginners, practising stake exercises has three functions: First of all, it prepares one psychologically for the practice. Calmness, relaxation and concentration are essential to the success in learning. Sore legs are inevitable. One must always be prepared to exert himself to overcome difficulties. Secondly, it prepares one for the special way of strength exertion. When practising *taijiquan*, the legs are always bent in a half-squat position. It takes some time for one to master this skill of exerting strength in such a motionless manner. And stakes aim at exercising the legs and can shorten this period. Thirdly, it helps one to keep a good posture of the upper body. A specific posture of the upper body is required in *taijiquan*, for example, lower the shoulders and elbows, hold back the chest and hips, etc. This posture is uncommon and unconscious in our daily life. Stake exercises turn it into

学练太极拳需付出艰苦努力的思想准备。第二,使初学者尽快适应练太极拳时腿部“静力性”的用劲方式。练习太极拳时,双腿几乎总要处于弯曲的半蹲状态。这种“静力性”的用劲方式初学者确实需要经过一定时间的适应才能习惯。“太极桩功”对腿部“静力性力量”的要求程度高于太极拳的动作和套路,可以直接提高腿部的“静力性力量”,缩短适应期。第三,使初学者尽快适应练习太极拳时的上体姿势。练习太极拳时,要求上肢和躯干要保持一定的形态,如“沉肩”、“垂肘”、“含胸”、“敛臀”等。这些上体姿势在日常生活中往往是无意识和不经常出现的。要使之成为有意识并能保持的体态,“太极桩功”是较好的方法,因为在站桩时可以有意识地体会和保持这些特殊体态,为学练和掌握太极拳的正确姿势与动作打好基础。根据简化太极拳的要求,我们进行下面几种站桩练习。

a. 平行步站桩。是“太极桩功”中的基本桩法。其姿势规格为,两脚平行开立与肩同宽;两腿屈蹲,身体重心落于两脚正中;躯干自然直立;两臂肘关节微曲抱于胸前如抱球状;双手掌心向内,指尖相对;手指自然微曲并展开;颈部自然竖直;头正,下颏微收,两眼平视前方。(图 1)其姿势要领为:两膝关节要微外撑,保持躯干的正直和身体重心的中正。学练该桩功初期,要特别注意不要一次站很长时间,一般每次 2~3 分钟即可,可多站几次,因站桩时间到 5 分钟不觉两腿酸痛时,学练太极拳效果较好。

one's established and conscious posture, leading the exerciser in learning and keeping this special posture purposefully. Stake exercises are classified as the following:

a. The stake of a parallel step

This is the basic stance of *taijiquan*.

图 1 **Fig** 1

Description: Stand with the two feet shoulder breadth, apart and parallel with the two legs bending, and the weight falling between the two feet; hold the body straight, with the arms embracing in front of the chest and the elbows slightly bending as if carrying a ball; keep the palms inward with the fingers relaxed, pointing one another; keep the head and neck upright, the eyes looking ahead, and the chin in. (Fig.1)

Main points: Keep the knees slightly outward to prop up the body so as to keep it upright. Do not attempt to stand too long at a time at the beginning. Two or three minutes would be adequate. If one does not get sore legs after standing like this for five minutes, one can count on an effective learning of *taijiquan*.

b. A bow-step stake

图 2 **Fig** 2

Description: Bend the fore leg to form a right angle with the ground, the knees not beyond the tiptoes; keep the rear leg straight, the tiptoes slightly outward; stand firmly with a parallel distance of 20 cm between the feet; drop the shoulders naturally with such a posture as in "Parting a Wild Horse's Mane" (Fig.2) or "Brushing the knees with a Twist Step" (Fig. 3); Keep the chin in and the head and neck straight, the eyes

b. 弓步站桩。是下肢保持弓步姿势的桩功练习。其姿势规格为：前腿屈膝半蹲，膝部不得超过脚尖；后腿髋关节自然内合，膝关节自然伸直，脚尖内扣斜前方约45°；两脚全脚掌着地，横向距离约20cm左右；上体自然正直，两臂可在身体两侧自然松肩下垂，也可摆成“野马分鬃”（图2）或“搂膝拗步”（图3）的上肢姿势；颈部自然竖直；头正，下颌微收，两眼平视前方。其姿势要领为：后脚掌外侧要内扣；髋关节要向下松沉。

图3　　Fig 3

注意两点：第一，在注意后脚外侧不离地的前提下，尽量加大弓步前后两脚的距离，以提高弓步的美观程度和腿部力量。第二，要注意上体及颈、头部的正直，保持正确姿势。并左右腿前后交替练习。

c. 虚步站桩。是下肢保持虚步姿势的桩功练习。其姿势规格为：后腿屈膝半蹲，全脚掌着地，脚尖斜朝前；前腿膝关节微屈，以脚尖或脚跟在身前点地；上体自然正直；两臂可摆成“白鹤亮翅”（图4）或“手挥琵琶”（图5）的上肢姿势；颈部自然竖直；头正，下颌微收，两眼平视前方。其姿势要点为：后腿支撑体重，前腿要“虚点”地面，两腿用劲要“虚实分明”。注意两点：第一，虚步是一腿支撑体重，支撑腿的负担较大，所以要在前两个站桩的基础上学练“虚步站桩”。第二，上体在支撑腿髋关节屈收的前提下注意保持正直，以培养单腿负担体重时的上体正确姿态。

looking ahead.

Main points: Drop the hips naturally. The rear foot should cling to the ground firmly. Make the step as large as possible so that it is more pleasing to the eye and more helpful for leg strength. Keep the upper part of the body upright so that it won't incline forward. Change the legs constantly for practice.

c. An empty-step stake

图 4 Fig 4

图 5 Fig 5

Description: Bend the rear leg with the sole on the ground and the tiptoe forward; slightly bend the front leg with either the tiptoe or the heel touching the ground; hold the upper part of the body upright; keep the chin in and the neck straight naturally, the eyes looking ahead. The posture of the arms is the same with that of " A White Crane Spreading Its Wings"(Fig.4) or"Playing a Pipa"(Fig.5).

Main points: The rear leg undertakes all the body weight. Do not lay any weight on the front leg. Try to feel the solidness and emptiness. Since one has to stand on one leg, practise the first two stakes before practising the empty-step stake. Though all the body weight is supported by one leg, do not forget to keep the upper body straight.

2. 循序渐进的学练方法

(1) 先外后内

外指的是肢体的外形动作。内指的是心理、意识及其他内在活动。先外后内就是先学练拳架，即按照拳谱上各式的名称，一式一式地把肢体的外形动作学会，然后再与心理、意识及其他内在活动相配合，做到内外相合。

(2) 先零后整

零指的是个体动作。整指的是全套动作或组合动作的连贯性。先零后整就是在学拳架时，每学一式，先把这一式的动作加以分解，化整为零，逐个学习。如学练揽雀尾一式可以把它分解为掤、捋、挤、按四个动作依次学习，做到方向对头、姿势正确以后，再把各个动作连贯起来。学会一式再学一式，每新学一个招式都把以前所学各式从头到尾复习一遍或多遍。

(3) 先下后上

下指的是下肢动作。上指的是上肢动作。先下后上就是每学一式，先学步型、步法，后学手型、手法。如学习野马分鬃可先学弓步的步型和步法，后学抱球、分掌。分别把上下姿势学会，立即配合练习，达到上下相随。

(4) 先直后曲

直指的是直线。曲指的是曲线。先直后曲就是初学太极拳动作时，手脚的运行可直来直去，也可有停顿，以求得方向对，落点准。随即把直线动作改为弧形、环形，并去掉停顿，做到圆和连贯。

2. A Step-by-Step Practising Method

(1) From the exterior to the interior

The exterior refers to the movements of the limbs. The interior refers to consciousness, mental activities, etc. "From the exterior to the interior" means that one should learn the basic frame of *taijiquan* first — to master the limb movements of every form. After this has been achieved, one should try to integrate the movements with one's mental thoughts and activities.

(2) From the separate to the whole

The separate refers to each move. The whole refers to the continuity of all the moves of the whole set. A form can be separated into several moves. For instance, the form "Grasping a Peacock's Tail" can be separated into 4 moves — parrying, brushing, pressing and pushing. Study and practise each move until all the postures are right and then practise them in a continued form. Do review all the forms learned previously before learning a new one

(3) From the lower to the upper

The lower refers to the legs and the upper refers to the arms. When one learns a form, one first pays attention to the stances and the basic steps, and then the handforms. For example, in learning the form "Parting a Wild Horse's Mane", one should learn the bow step first, followed by "Carrying a Ball" or "Parting the Palms" before he learns to match the steps with the handforms.

(4) From straight to curve

For beginners, straight movements and pauses in the actions are allowed to seek correct direction and accurate location of every movement. As soon as one is familiar with the straight movements, one should change them into curves and circles and eliminate the pauses to maintain continuity.

(5) 先临摹后自修

临摹就是请人教,照着别人的样子做。自修就是看书,看图,自己练习提高,因为有些细微的动作在书上很难看到看准。先临摹后自修最好是临摹一式两式,立即自修,否则,一旦动作定型就难以改正或提高。

(6) 要持之以恒

学练太极拳不是一天的功夫,必须持之以恒。做到天天练,长期练,这样才能不断学习,不断提高,精益求精。达到防病、除病、健脑、健身的目的。否则,忽冷忽热,三天打鱼两天晒网,想练就练,想停就停,成效不会大。

(5) From imitation to self-study

Imitation is to learn from a teacher and do as the teacher does. Self-study includes study of the books and illustrations, self-practice, etc. Some movements scarcely perceptible are hard to get when reading books. Therefore, one should first imitate one form or two, and then practise at once. It is much more difficult to correct one's movements if one has established the false way of moving.

(6) Practising perseveringly

Taijiquan will not be mastered in one day. To learn *taijiquan* well, one must practise every day over a long period of time. This is the only way to make progress. One will not have much gains if one works by fits and starts.

第二章　太极拳运动的技术

Chapter Two: The Working Mechanism of Taijiquan

一、24式太极拳基本技术的规格要领

1. 手型

图6　　Fig 6

(1) 拳

五指蜷屈，大拇指压于食指、中指第二指节上。拳面要平，握拳不可太紧。(图6)

(2) 掌

五指自然伸直，虎口成弧形，手指不可僵直。(图7)

(3) 勾

五指第一指节捏拢，屈腕，勾尖朝下，手指和腕部都要松活自然。也可拇指和食指、中指捏拢，无名指和小指屈于掌心。(图8)

图7　　Fig 7

图8　　Fig 8

2. 手法

(1) 掤

手臂成弧形，由下向前上顶架，高与肩平，掌心向内，着力点在小臂外侧中上部，肘关节稍低于手。手指既不可软弱无力，也不可僵硬挺直。(图9、10)

Ⅰ. The Technical Specifications of 24-Form *Taijiquan*

1. Basic Handforms

(1) A fist: The hand is clenched with the fingers doubled into the palm and the thumb doubled inward across the second knuckles of the forefinger and the middle finger to make a fist. The fist should be clenched loosely and the wrist should be relaxed and flat. (Fig.6)

(2) A palm: The fingers are stretched and separated naturally to form a curve between the thumb and the index finger. The fingers should not be stiffly straight. (Fig.7)

(3) A hook: Keep the first knuckles of the five fingers naturally together and bend the wrist, pointing the hook downward. Pay attention to the flexibility of the fingers and the wrist. One can also form a hook with only three fingers, leaving the ring finger and the little finger doubled into the palm. (Fig.8)

2. Basic Techniques of Hand Movements

(1) Upward and outward parrying

The arm is bent, with the palm inward; move the arm up from below for an upward parry to the shoulder's height, with the force at the outer side of the forearm and the fingers neither forceless nor stiffly straight. (Fig.9 & 10)

图 9 **Fig 9**

图 10 **Fig 10**

(2) 捋

两臂微屈,掌心斜相对,随腰的转动,由前向侧后划弧拉带,动作必须走弧形曲线,不可直拉直抽。(图 11、12)

图 11　Fig 11

图 12　Fig 12

(3) 挤

前手臂屈肘直腕,后手坐腕贴近前手,腕部内侧帮助向前顶出;顶出后两臂撑圆,高不过肩、低不过胸。在做挤时要弓步拧腰协调一致。(图 13、14)

图 13　Fig 13

图 14　Fig 14

(4) 按

两臂屈曲而伸,由后向前上方推出,路线:先向下引再向前上方用力,不可直推。推时掌心朝前,指尖朝上,臂微屈,肘部松沉,指高不过肩。按掌时要与向前弓步协调一致。(图 15、16)

(2) Downward parrying with both hands

The palms face each other, and the arms slightly bent; move the hands backward while turning the waist. The move should follow a curve. (Fig.11 & 12)

(3) Pushing with circled arms

Keep the front arm curved with the wrist straight, and the palm of the rear arm close to the inner side of the front forearm, with the palm facing forward and the fingers up; push both hands forward, with the arms forming a circle between the chest and the shoulders. The hand movements should go with the bow step and waist turning. (Fig. 13 & 14)

(4) Pressing

Press both arms forward in a circular shape with the palms forward and the fingers up; bend the arms slightly and drop the elbows. Do not press directly forward — press a little bit downward first, then upward. The fingers should not be higher than the shoulders. The pressing should be well coordinated with the step. (Fig. 15 & 16)

图 15　　**Fig 15**

图 16　　**Fig 16**

(5) 冲拳

拳从腰间旋转向前打出成立拳，臂微屈，肘不要僵直。（图 17、18）

图 17　Fig 17

图 18　Fig 18

(6) 贯拳

拳从侧下方向斜上方弧形横打；臂微屈，拳眼斜向下，着力点在拳面。（图 19、20）

图 19　Fig 19

图 20　Fig 20

(7) 抱掌

两掌心上下相对，在体前或体侧成抱球状；上手高不过肩，下手约在小腹部位，两掌撑圆，两臂成弧形，同时松肩垂肘。（图 21、22）

(5) A hitting fist

Hit forward with the fist from behind, with the fist eye (the round hole formed by the thumb and the forefinger) up. Bend the arm slightly. The elbow should not be stiff. (Fig. 17 & 18)

(6) A swinging punch

Swing the fists obliquely upward in a circular shape from the sides below. Bend the arms slightly with the fist eyes slantingly downward and the force at the fists' faces. (Fig. 19 & 20)

(7) An upper palm block

The palms face each other, one upward, the other downward; keep the arms in a circle for a firm block in front of the body or at the side of the body. The upper hand should be levelled with the chest, while the lower hand at the height of the abdomen. Drop the shoulders and the elbows. (Fig.21 & 22)

图 21 **Fig 21**

图 22 **Fig 22**

(8) 分掌

两掌由合抱向前后或左右分开，两臂微屈成弧形（图 23、24）

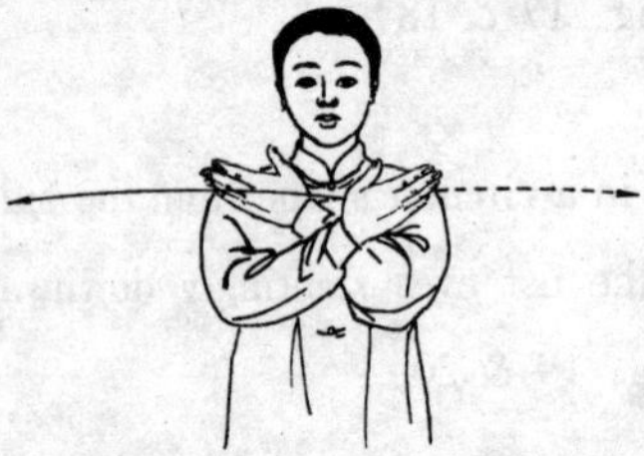

图 23　Fig 23

图 24　Fig 24

(9) 格掌

掌内旋，掌心朝向自己，从面或胸的外侧向内侧运动，力点在掌的外侧或小臂的外侧，以格挡敌人对面部或胸部的攻击。（图 25）

图 25　Fig 25

(10) 搂掌

掌心向下，从身体异侧经体前运动至身体同侧，做格拨动作，停止时，掌心向下，掌指朝前。（图 26）

(8) Parting palms

Part the crossed or linked hands and move them to both sides; keep the hands in opposite directions after the separation; bend the arms slightly to form a curve. (Fig. 23 & 24)

(9) A blocking palm

Move both hands inward in front of the chest with the palms facing the chest. Force should be generated from the outer side of the palm and forearm to block against the opponent's attack on the face or the chest. (Fig. 25)

(10) A gathering palm

Move one hand from one side of the body to the other as if gathering something with the arm, the palm facing downward and the fingers forward. (Fig. 26)

图 26 Fig 26

(11) 推掌

掌从肩上、腰间或胸部沿中线向前运动。出击臂微屈呈弧形，掌心向前，指高不过头。(图 27、28)

图 27　　Fig 27

图 28　　Fig 28

(12) 穿掌

掌沿另一手臂或大腿内侧伸出，掌指朝向运动方向。(图 29、30)

图 29　　Fig 29

图 30　　Fig 30

(13) 云手

两掌在体前交叉向两侧划立圆。掌高不过头，低不过裆，两掌在体侧上下交换。(图 31 ~ 35)

(11) Pushing

Extend the hand forward from the shoulder, the waist or the chest. The pushing should be executed along the central line of the body, and not too inclined to one side. The arm is bent slightly with the palm forward and the fingers no higher than the head. (Fig. 27 & 28)

(12) A shuttling palm

Extend one palm along the other arm or inner side of the other leg, the fingers pointing to the moving direction. (Fig. 29 & 30)

(13) Waving hands like clouds

Cross the two palms in front of the chest and then move to the sides to draw circles. Keep the palms no higher than the head and no lower than the crotch. The height of the two palms are alternated at the side of the body. (Fig.31 – 35)

图 31 Fig 31

图 32 Fig 32

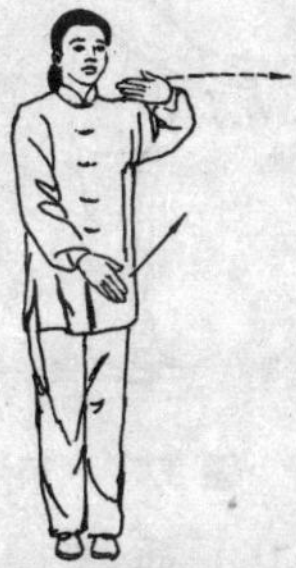

图 33 Fig 33

图 34 Fig 34

图 35 Fig 35

(14) 架掌

屈臂上举，掌位于头前上方，掌心斜向外。（图 36）

图 36 Fig 36

(15) 挑掌

侧掌由下向上方抬起，指尖向上，力点在掌的拇指一侧。（图 37、38）

图 37 Fig 37

图 38 Fig 38

(16) 插掌

四指伸直并拢，拇指自然分开，臂由屈而伸，掌沿指尖方向伸出，力点在指尖。（图 39、40）

3. 步型

(1) 弓步

两脚前后开立，前腿屈膝，大腿成水平，膝关节与脚尖接近垂直，前脚尖朝前；后腿自然蹬直，后脚尖斜向约 45°，两脚均全脚掌着地，宽度为 10～30 公分。（图 41）

(14) A sustaining palm

Bend the arm and raise it to the top of the head with the palm outward. (Fig. 36)

(15) A poking palm

Raise the palm upward from the side of the body with the fingers upward. The force should be generated from the thumb. (Fig. 37 & 38)

(16) An inserting palm

Keep the thumb separated from the four fingers. Bend the arm and then stretch it. Reach out the palm in the direction of the fingers, with the force at the fingertips. (Fig. 39 & 40)

图 39 **Fig** 39

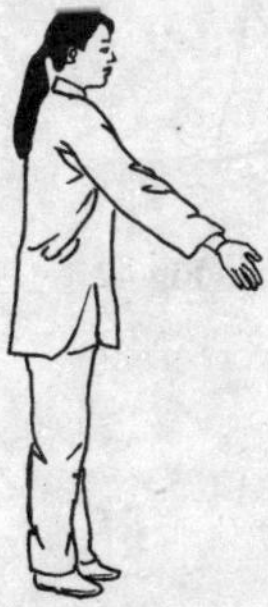

图 40 **Fig** 40

3. Basic Stances

(1) A bow step

图 41 **Fig** 41

Keep the legs apart, one behind the other; bend the front leg so that the knee is right above the tiptoes and keep the rear leg naturally straight. The tiptoes of the front foot point forward, and those of the rear foot sideways with a 45° angle. Both feet stand firmly on the ground with a distance of 10 to 30 cm between them. (Fig. 41)

(2) 虚步

后腿屈膝半蹲，大腿接近水平。脚跟与臀部基本垂直，脚尖稍向外展，全脚掌着地；前腿微屈前伸，前脚掌或脚跟轻轻点地。（图 42、43）

图 42　Fig 42

图 43　Fig 43

(3) 仆步

一腿全蹲，全脚着地，脚尖稍外展，另一腿自然伸直于体侧，接近地面，脚尖内扣，全脚掌着地，置于全蹲腿的脚跟的侧直线上。（图 44）

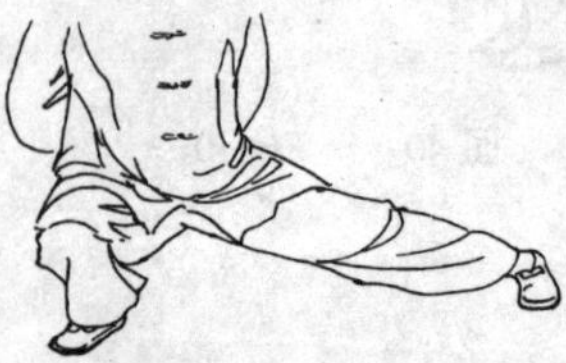

图 44　Fig 44

(4) 独立步

支撑腿接近直立，另一腿屈膝提起于体前，大腿高于水平，上体直立。（图 45）

(5) 丁步

两腿半蹲并拢，一脚全脚掌着地支撑，另一脚与支撑脚内侧相靠，脚尖点地。（图 46）

(2) An empty step

Keep the feet apart, one in front of the other; bend the rear leg and squat with the thigh at horizontal level, forming a vertical line between the heel and the buttocks; keep the rear foot on the ground firmly and the tiptoes outward, while the heel or tiptoes of the front foot touching the ground lightly. (Fig. 42 & 43)

(3) A crouch stance

Bend one leg and fully squat with the tiptoes outward; keep the other leg naturally straight and press it down close to the ground with the tiptoes forward and slightly inward, forming a straight line with the heel of the squatted leg. (Fig. 44)

(4) A single-leg step

Stand on one leg and raise the other with the knee bent and the thigh above horizontal level; keep the upper part of the body upright. (Fig. 45)

图 45　　**Fig** 45

图 46　　**Fig** 46

(5) A "T" step

Keep the legs together and stand half squat with one foot firmly on the ground and the other close to the supporting foot with the heel off. (Fig.46)

(6) 马步

两脚左右开立约为脚长的三至四倍，脚尖正对前方，屈膝半蹲，大腿成水平。（图 47）

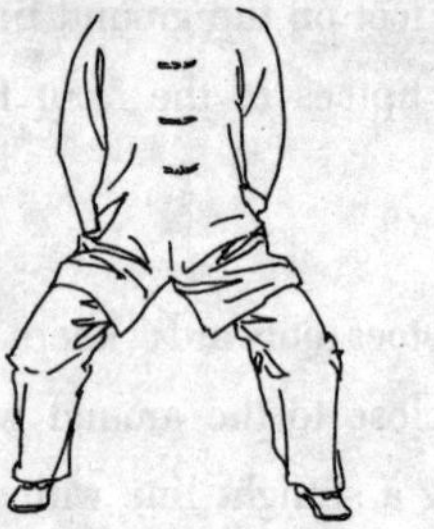

图 47　Fig 47

图 48　Fig 48

4. 步法

(1) 上步

后脚向前进一步或半步，或前脚前移半步。（图 48）

(2) 退步

前脚后移退一步。（图 49、50）

图 49　Fig 49

图 50　Fig 50

(3) 跟步

后脚向前靠进半步。（图 51、52）

(6) A horse-riding step

Keep the feet apart with a distance of three to four times the length of the foot with the tiptoes forward; squat until the thighs reach the horizontal level.(Fig.47)

4. Basic Steps

(1) Advancing

Move the front foot half a step forward or move the rear foot a step forward, passing the front foot. (Fig.48)

(2) Retreating

Move the front foot a step backward. (Fig. 49 & 50)

(3) A follow-up step

Move the rear foot half a step forward, but still behind the front foot.(Fig.51 & 52)

图 51　　Fig 51

图 52　　Fig 52

(4) 侧行步

两脚平行连续侧向移动。(图 53~55)

图 53 Fig 53

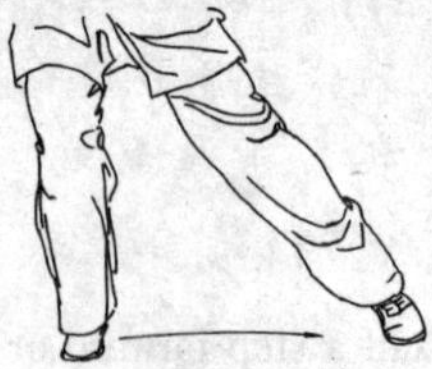

图 54 Fig 54

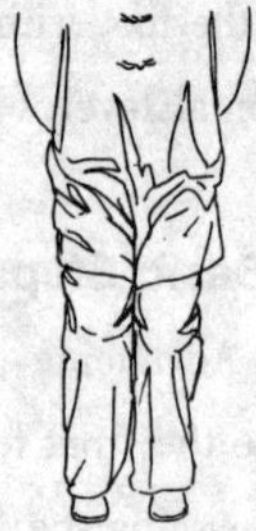

图 55 Fig 55

5. 腿法

蹬腿

支撑腿接近直立,另一腿屈膝提起,而后脚慢慢蹬出,腿伸直,脚尖上勾,脚高过腰部,力点在脚跟。(图 56、57)

6. 身型身法

(1) 头颈

头部自然上顶,头颈勿左右歪斜前俯后仰,颈肌勿僵直。头颈动作应随身体沿纵轴转动,与躯干的旋转上下协调一致。初学者头部只要做到轻轻上顶、下颏微收、头部摆正、头颈将腰背轻轻领起即可。这也就是俗称的"虚颏顶劲。"

对面部的要求是放松自然,口自然闭合或微微张开,牙齿轻轻咬合,舌自然平放或舌尖抵上腭,用鼻呼吸。眼神随身体的转动注视前手或平视前方(个别时候

(4) A side step

Move the feet to either side continuously with the tiptoes always forward. (Fig. 53 - 55)

5. Basic Leg Technique

Kick

Stand on one leg; raise the other with the knee bent; slowly kick out the raised leg until the leg is straight and the foot is above the waist level. The force should come from the heel and tiptoes upward. (Fig. 56 & 57)

图 56　　**Fig 56**

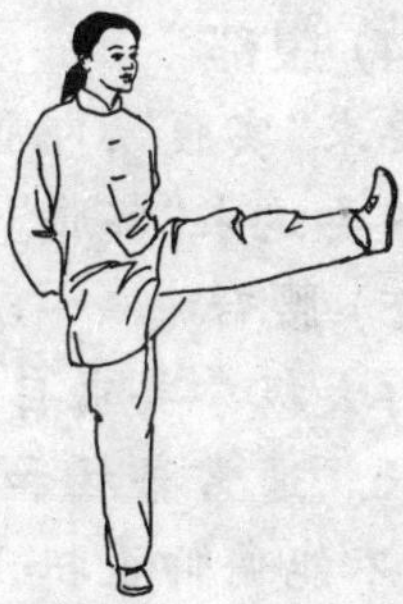

图 57　　**Fig 57**

6. Basic Requirements of the Body

(1) The head and the neck

The head is up and the neck is vertical but not stiff. They should turn with the turning of the body. A beginner should raise his/her head to lead the moving of the waist and back. The face should be relaxed with the chin in.

The face is naturally relaxed. The teeth are clenched and the mouth either close naturally or open slightly, the tongue either lying flat

看后手)。神态自然,注意力集中。

(2) 肩肘

要求"沉肩坠肘",即肩关节要保持松沉,不可耸沉。肘关节要保持自然弯曲,并轻微下沉,不能抬肘直臂,从而达到自然、沉稳、柔和的要求。

(3) 胸背

要求"含胸拔背",即胸不外挺,两臂微内含,胸部肌肉放松,脊背舒展自然,胸部松开,除去肋间肌紧张,使呼吸自然舒畅,利于血液回流心脏。

(4) 腹部

要求"实腹",即腹部要做到放松,使呼吸沉长。初学者不要追求"实腹"的感觉而使腹肌紧张。

(5) 腰脊

打太极拳要求自身中正,即直腰,并且腰肌松活,不可紧张。通常脊柱和腰部是沿上下轴转动带动肢体运动,而不能俯仰歪扭,从而使腰部的运动灵活自然,全身协调一致地运动。

(6) 腿胯

在打太极拳时,不管是弓步、虚步还是仆步,常常是一腿弯曲,另一腿自然伸直。弯曲腿承担大部分体重。在步法转换中,两腿的屈伸转换是随时进行的。为了使身体姿势中正平衡,必须要保持屈腿落胯(即身体好似自然地坐落在支撑身体的腿上)。两腿几乎不能有同时站直的时候,以免造成身体忽高忽低。正确的步法变换除了注意腿部姿势外,还必须运转腰胯,即俗称"步随身换"。不会运用腰胯动作就会生硬,上下运动就不协调。

or reaching the upper palate. Breathe with the nose only. The eyes should look ahead or follow the movements of the fore hand (occasionally those of the rear hand), and the mind should concentrate.

(2) The shoulders and the elbows

The shoulders should be dropped, but not shrugged. The elbows are naturally bent and lowered, but should not be stiffly straight.

(3) The chest and the back

Keep the chest in and fully extend the back; relax the muscles to smooth the breath. It will help the blood to flow back to the heart and to nourish the internal organs to the maximum extent.

(4) The abdomen

Taijiquan requires a "firm abdomen". It does not mean to stiffen the abdominal muscles. It calls for relaxation of the belly which ensures long and deep breath.

(5) The waist and the spine

The waist, which links the upper and the lower parts of the body, should be straight but flexible. Keep the spine and the waist on a vertical line. The turning of the waist and spine leads the movements of the limbs. Keep the movements of every part of the body harmonious.

(6) The legs and the hips

When practising the bow step, the empty step and the crouch step, practitioners should always keep one leg bent and the other naturally straight. The bent leg undertakes most of the weight. In the change of steps, the legs are constantly changing between empty and solid. Relax the hips to rest the body on the supporting leg. Don't stand straight on both feet, as it will make one look tall one minute and short the next. Steps are changed to the turning of the body, so inappropriate movements of the waist and hips will lead to clumsy and inconsistent movements on the whole.

二、24式太极拳的组合动作

1. 白鹤亮翅接搂膝拗步

手分解动作

(1) 以腰为轴上体微向左转,同时右手向左摆至体前,由体前下落,随之身体向右转,经胯侧再向右后上方划弧与肩高,手心向上,眼看右手。

(2) 右手下落时,左手开始外旋翻转,左手由胯侧向上经面前再向右划弧至右肩前,肘部略低于腕部,手心向下。

(3) 上体稍左转,右臂屈肘,右手收至右耳侧,虎口对耳,掌心斜向前;左手下落至右腹前,手心向下,眼看前方。

(4) 右手从耳侧向前推出,手指尖与鼻尖平,推掌时沉肩微垂肘,推到顶点时要坐腕、展掌、舒指;左手继续向前、向下、向左划弧由膝前搂过,按在左胯侧稍偏前,手心向下,指尖朝前,坐腕、展掌、舒指,眼看右手。

脚分解动作

(1) 左虚步变为左脚收至右脚内侧,脚尖点地,身体重心在右腿。

(2) 右腿保持原屈膝程度,身体重心仍在右腿上,随转体左脚向左前侧方迈出一步,左腿自然伸直,脚跟着地,两脚跟横向距离约30公分。

(3) 上体继续左转至面向前方,左脚踏实,左腿屈弓;右腿自然伸直成左弓步,身体重心主要移至左腿,上

Ⅱ. The Combination Movements of 24-Form *Taijiquan*

1. "A White Crane Spreading Its Wings", Followed by "Brushing the Knees and Twisting the Steps on Both Sides"

Illustrations of the hand movements

(1) With the waist as the axis, turn the torso slightly to the left. Meanwhile, move the right hand left to the front of the body. And then, while turning the torso to the right, move the right hand in a curved line, palm up, downward in front of the body, passing the side of the hip and up behind the back until it reaches shoulder level. Keep the eyes on the right hand.

(2) When the right hand moves downward, the left hand begins to turn over outwardly. The left hand moves from the side of the hip to the front of the head and curves rightward in front of the right shoulder, with the elbow slightly lower than the wrist and the palm facing downward.

(3) Slightly turn the body to the left. Bend the right arm and the right hand must be beside the right ear. The part of the hand between the thumb and the index finger faces towards the ear. The palm slants to the front. The left hand falls down to the right side in front of the abdomen with the palm facing downward and the eyes looking forward.

(4) Push the right hand downward from the side of the ear. The fingertips and the nose tip are almost at the same height. When one is pushing the hand, drop the shoulder and elbow slightly. Open and stand the palm, extend the fingers while pushing to the utmost. Curve

体正直，松腰松胯。

手脚配合

(1) 以腰为轴上体微转，两手划弧到右侧时收脚。（图 58）

图 58　Fig 58

(2) 屈臂出左脚。（图 59）

图 59　Fig 59

图 60　Fig 60

(3) 搂膝推掌。（图 60）

2. 搂膝拗步接手挥琵琶

手分解动作

(1) 上体右转，左手向左、向上划弧摆至体前，手臂

the left hand forward and push downward to the left, past the knee. Keep the left hand to the side of the left hip, slightly to the front, with the palm downward and the fingertips forward. Open and stand the palm, extend the fingers and focus the eyes on the right hand.

Illustrations of the leg movements

(1) Change the left empty step to the position of the left foot, stopping at the inner side of the right foot. Put the left foot on the ground on tiptoes — the body weight is now on the right leg.

(2) Hold the right leg bending as beforc. The weight is still on the right leg. While turning the torso, step forward with the left leg and stretch it naturally. The heel must be on the ground. The parallel distance between the two heels is about 30cm.

(3) The body continues to turn left until facing forward. The left foot is solid and the left leg is bending. Stretch the right leg naturally to form a left bow step. The weight is mainly on the left leg, with an erect body and a loose waist and hips.

Coordination of the hands and the legs

(1) With the waist as the axis, turn the body slightly. Move the hands in curved lines to the right side of the body, and simultaneously withdraw the foot back beside the other. (Fig. 58)

(2) Bend the arm and stretch the left foot. (Fig.59)

(3) Brush the knee with the left hand and push the right hand forward. (Fig.60)

2. "Brush the Knees and Twisting the Steps on Both Sides", Followed by "Playing the Lute"

Illustrations of the hand movements

(1) Turn the body to the right. The left hand moves to the left

自然伸直，掌心斜向下；右手屈臂后引，收至胸前，掌心斜向下，眼看右手。

(2) 上体稍向左回转，两臂外旋，同时侧掌合手体前，左手心向右，高与鼻平；右手合在左前臂里侧，右手心与左肘相对，两臂屈肘，眼看左手。

脚分解动作

(1) 身体重心移至左腿，右脚向前跟半步，前脚掌着地。

(2) 右脚全脚掌踏实，身体后坐，重心移至右腿，随右脚踏实，上体稍右转，左脚跟离地。

(3) 左脚稍向前移，脚跟着地，膝部微屈，成左虚步，上体正直，松腰松胯。

手脚配合

(1) 右脚上前半步，右臂稍向前伸。（图 61）

(2) 后坐引手，上体右转，两臂同时完成。（图 62）

图 61　Fig 61

图 62　Fig 62

and then up along a curving route and stops in front of the body. Stretch the left arm naturally with the palm slanting downward. Bend the right arm and move the right hand from the back and stop in front of the chest with the palm slanting down and the eyes on the right hand.

(2) Turn the body back slightly, with the arms open. Put the two palms together in front of the body with the fingers pointing forward. The left palm faces the right at nose level. Put the right hand at the inner side of the left arm with the right palm facing the left elbow, bending both arms with the eyes on the left hand.

Illustrations of the leg movements

(1) Shift the weight to the left leg, take a forward half-step of the right leg, and put the foresole on the ground.

(2) Make the right foot solid, sit back the body and the weight should now be shifted to the right leg. As the right foot is made solid, turn the body slightly to the right and hold the heel of the left foot just above the ground.

(3) Move the left foot slightly forward with the left heel on the ground. Bend the left knee slightly to form a left empty step with an erect body and a loose waist and hips.

Coordination of the hands and the legs

(1) Make a forward half-step of the right leg and slightly stretch the right arm forward. (Fig. 61)

(2) Sit back and move the hands. Turn the body to the right and finish the movements of the two arms at the same time. (Fig. 62)

(3) 两臂合拢时，左手臂大于 90°，右手放在左肘旁。同时成左虚步。(图 63)

图 63　　**Fig 63**

3. 倒卷肱接揽雀尾

手分解动作

(1) 上体微向右转，同时右手由胯侧向右后上方划弧举至与肩同高，手心向上，肘部微屈；左手在体前放松成手心向下，两臂约成侧平状。上体继续右转，右臂向胸前平屈，手心翻转向下；左前臂外旋，左手由体前划弧下落至右腹前，手心向上，两手上下相对成抱球状。(图 64、65)

(3) When the two arms are closed, the angle of the left arm is over 90°, with the right hand against the left elbow. Simultaneously, form a left empty step. (Fig.63)

3. "Curving Back Arms on Both Sides", Followed by "Grasping a Peacock's Tail"

Illustrations of the hand movements

(1) Turn the body slightly to the right. Meanwhile, the right hand curves from the side of the hip to the upper back and stop at the shoulder level with the palm up. The arm must be slightly bent. Put the left hand loose in front of the body and turn the palm downward. The two arms are at about the same level. Continue to turn the body to the right. Balance the right hand in front of the chest with the palm facing downward. Swing the left forearm outward from the front of the body to the front of the right abdomen with the palm facing upward. Form the two hands into a ball, with the palms facing each other. (Fig. 64 & 65)

图 64 **Fig** 64

图 65 **Fig** 65

(2) 上体微向左转至前方，两手开始左上右下分开，上体正直，左臂平屈弧形，肘部略低于腕部，向体前掤出，腕与胸相对，手心向里；右手向右下方划弧落按于右胯旁，手心向下，四指朝前，坐腕、舒指、眼看左腕。(图 66)

(3) 上体微左转，随转体左臂内旋，左手向左前方伸出，手心斜向下；右前臂外旋，右手经腹前向上向左前伸至左前臂里侧，手心斜向上。(图 67)

图 66　Fig 66

图 67　Fig 67

(4) 上体向右转，同时随转体两手向下向右划弧后捋，右手摆至身体右后方，手心向上，高与肩平；左手屈收于右肩前，手心向里，眼看右手。(图 68)

图 68　Fig 68

(5) 上体左转面向前方，右臂屈收于体前，右手搭于左腕内侧，手心向前；左手横向内，高与胸平。(图 69)

(2) Turn the body slightly from the left to the front. The two hands begin to split apart, the left one upward while the right one downward. At this time, keep the body erect and bend the left arm to form a horizontal curve. The elbow is a little lower than the wrist. Raise the left arm forward with the left wrist facing the chest and the left palm inward. Swing the right hand down and draw it back beside the right hip, with the palm facing downward and the fingers (but not the thumb) pointing forward. Stand the right hand and extend the fingers, the eyes looking at the left wrist. (Fig.66)

(3) As the torso turns slightly to the left, twist the left arm inward, then stretch the right hand forward and slant its palm downward. Twist the right arm outward, the right hand past the front of the abdomen. Then stretch the hand up and then forward to the inner side of the left arm and slant its palm upward. (Fig. 67)

(4) Turn the upper body to the right. At the same time, stroke the left hand downward along a curved line to the back, then bend it and draw it back in front of the right shoulder, with the palm facing inward, and swing the right hand toward the back right, with the palm up to shoulder level and keep the eyes on the right hand. (Fig. 68)

(5) Turn the body to the left and look forward. Draw the right arm back to the front of the torso. Grasp the inner left wrist loosely, palm forward. Balance the left arm at chest level. (Fig.69)

图 69　　**Fig** 69

(6) 两臂由屈而伸向前挤出，挤出后两臂撑圆，高与肩平，眼看前方。(图 70)

图 70　Fig 70

图 71　Fig 71

(7) 左前臂内旋，左手向下翻掌，右手手心转向下，经左腕上方向前伸出，随之两手左右分开，与肩同宽，两臂屈收后引至胸前，两手心向前下方。(图 71)

(8) 上体正直，松腰松胯，两手经腹前沿弧线向前按出，与肩同宽，手心均向前，按到顶点时腕部高与肩平，两肘微屈，坐腕，舒指，眼看前方。(图 72、73)

脚分解动作

(1) 左脚收右脚内侧，脚尖点地，上体微左转，向左前方迈出一步，脚跟落地；重心前移，左脚踏实，右腿自然伸直，左腿屈膝前弓，成左弓步。

(2) 上体右转，重心后移，身体后坐，右腿屈膝，左腿自然伸直。

(6) Press and stretch the two bending arms to form a circle at shoulder level and look forward. (Fig.70)

(7) Twist the left forearm in and then turn the palms downward. When the right hand passes over the left wrist, stretch it forward. Then keep the two hands at about shoulder width apart. Bend the two arms and draw them back in front of the chest with the palms facing outwards. (Fig.71)

(8) With an erect body, a loose waist and hips, push the hands past the abdomen along a curved line with the two arms about shoulder width apart and with the palms forward. When the hands reach their limits, bend the elbows a little, stand the wrists at shoulder level, extend the fingers and look forward. (Fig.72 & 73)

图 72　　**Fig** 72

图 73　　**Fig** 73

Illustrations of the leg movements

(1) Draw the left foot to the inner side of the right foot, with the toes on the ground. Turn the torso slightly to the left and step forward to the left, with the heel on the ground, shift the weight forward and make the left foot solid. Stretch the right leg naturally and bend the left knee to form a left bow step.

(2) Turn the body to the right and shift the weight backward. Squat and bend the right knee, and stretch the left leg naturally.

（3）重心前移，左腿屈弓，右腿自然蹬直成左弓步；重心后移，上体后坐，右腿屈膝，左腿自然伸直，左脚尖翘起；重心后移，左脚踏实，左腿屈弓，右腿自然蹬直成左弓步。

手脚配合

（1）收脚抱球，弓步分手。

（2）掤捋挤按时上下肢协调配合。

（3）两个揽雀尾弓步横向距离约10公分。

4. 揽雀尾接单鞭

手分解动作

（1）随转体左手手心向外，虎口向右经面前向左划弧至身体左侧，手心向左指尖朝上，肘微下垂；右手经腹前向左划弧至左肋前，手心向内，眼看左手。（图74、75）

图 74　　Fig 74

图 75　　Fig 75

(3) Shift the weight forward. Bend the left leg like a bow and stretch the right leg with some efforts to form a left bow step. Shift the weight backward, squat, bend the right knee and stretch the left leg naturally, with the toes pointing up. Then continue to shift the weight backward and make the left foot solid. Bend the left leg and stretch the right leg naturally to form a left bow step.

Coordination of the hands and the legs

(1) Draw the foot and make an "embracing ball" of the hands. Take a bow step and part the hands.

(2) The arms and legs should coordinate harmoniously when the hands make a raising, stroking, pressing or pushing movement.

(3) Keep a parallel distance of about 10cm between the feet in the two bow steps in the movement of "Grasping a Peacock's Tail".

4. "Grasping a Peacock's Tail" Followed by "Single Whip"

Illustrations of the hand movements

(1) While turning the torso, with the palm outward and the part between the thumb and the index finger toward the right, move the left hand past the face along a curved line, and stop it at the left side of the body, with the palm facing the left and the fingers pointing up. Take care to drop the elbow slightly. Move the right hand to the left and stop in front of the left ribs, with the palm facing inward and the eyes looking at the left hand. (Fig.74 & 75)

(2) 右手随转体向右经头前划弧,手心由向内逐渐翻转向外,经面前至身体右侧变勾手,腕高与肩平,肘微下垂;左手向下经腹前向右上划弧,手心逐渐转向里,最后停于右肩前。(图 76)

图 76　　Fig 76

图 77　　Fig 77

(3) 上体微向左转,左手随转体经面前向左划弧,左掌慢慢翻转向前推出,手心向前,腕与肩高,沉肩垂肘,左肘和左膝、左脚尖上下相对,眼看左手。(图 77)

脚分解动作

(1) 左腿屈膝,上体后坐,身体重心逐渐移至右腿,右脚尖尽量里扣。(图 78)

(2) 上体左转,右腿屈膝,身体重心移至右腿,左脚收至右脚里侧,脚尖点地。(图 79)

图 78　　Fig 78

手脚配合

(1) 转体扣脚需同时,两臂交叉划弧右手心向内,左手心向外。

(2) Move the right hand along a curved line past the head while turning the torso. At the same time, turn the palm gradually from inward to outward, past the face and to the right side of the body. Form a hook hand, with the wrist at shoulder level. Drop the elbow slightly. Curve the left hand past the abdomen toward the upper right, turn the left palm gradually inward, and finally stop it in front of the right shoulder. (Fig. 76)

(3) Slightly turn the upper body to the left. As the torso turns, move the left hand along a curved route to the left, past the face. Gradually turn over the left palm and push, palm forward, with the wrist at shoulder level, and drop the shoulder and elbow. The left elbow should face the left knee and the left toes, and the eyes should look at the left hand. (Fig. 77)

Illustrations of the leg movements

(1) Bend the left knee, squat, shift the weight gradually to the right leg. Turn the right foot inward as much as possible. (Fig. 78)

(2) Turn the body to the left. Bend the right leg and shift the weight gradually to the right leg. Draw the left foot to the inner side of the right foot, and keep the toes on the ground. (Fig. 79)

图 79　　**Fig** 79

Coordination of the hands and the legs

(1) Turn the body and the foot inward at the same time. Curve and cross the two arms, with the right palm facing inward and the left palm facing outward.

(2) Coordinate the hands and legs harmoniously while turning the body and stepping forward. The two feet should not stand on the same line. The hook hand is at shoulder level.

(2) 转体上步时上下肢协调配合，左右脚不能在一条线上，勾手高度与肩同高。

5. 单鞭接云手

在练习中强调学生以腰为轴，以腰带臂。反复练习手臂动作，再练习脚的动作。

手分解动作

(1) 左手向下经腹前划弧，掌心由向体前随转体逐渐转腕翻掌，向上向右划弧至右肩前，掌心向内；右勾手变掌，掌心向外，沉肩垂肘、坐腕、舒指。

(2) 随转体左手手心向里经面前划弧至身体左侧，保持屈肘，手心斜向里，指尖高与鼻平；左手翻掌外撑，腕与肩平，沉肩垂肘，舒指；右手向下划弧至腹前，掌心由向右逐渐翻转向内，继续向左划弧至左肩前，手心向内，眼看左手。

脚分解动作

(1) 右腿屈膝后坐，上体右转，左脚尖内扣。

(2) 上体左转，右腿屈膝，重心移向左腿，右脚跟先离地，随上体继续向左转，身体重心继续左移，最后完全移至左腿，右前脚掌轻轻提起，收向左脚内侧，前脚掌先着地，全脚掌再踏实，脚尖与膝上下相对，两腿保持屈膝状态，两脚相距 10 至 20 厘米。

5. "Single Whip" Followed by "Waving Hands like Clouds"

In practising, one should pay special attention to the movement of the waist, which moves like an axis and leads the movements of the arms. And also, practise the movements of the arms repeatedly before practising the movements of the legs.

Illustrations of the hand movements

(1) Move the left hand along a curved route downward, past the abdomen. As the body turns, start to turn the palm over gradually. When the palm faces the body, move the left hand along a curved route upward toward the right and stop it in front of the right shoulder. The palm must face inward. Change the right hook hand into palm facing outward and drop the shoulder and elbow. Stand the wrist and open the fingers.

(2) When the left palm turns inward, as the body turns, start to curve the left arm, the left hand past the face and stopping at the left side of the body. Keep the elbow bent, with the palm slanted inward and the fingertips at nose lovel. Turn over the left palm and extend it outward. Keep the wrist at shoulder level. Drop the shoulder and elbow and open the fingers. Curve the right arm downward, the right hand moving to the front of the abdomen. Turn the palm over, move it from facing to the right to facing inward, and continue to curve to the left and stop the right hand in front of the left shoulder, with the palm facing inward and the eyes looking at the left hand.

Illustrations of the leg movements

(1) Bend the right leg and squat. Turn the body to the right and turn the left toes inward.

(2) Turn the body to the left, bend the right knee and move the

手脚配合

(1) 左翻掌时出脚。

(2) 右翻掌时收脚。

(3) 两臂划弧运转时,手臂不可伸直。

(4) 云手的步是侧行步,要点起点落,轻起轻落,两脚虚实要分明,并步时膝稍内扣,脚尖不可成八字形。

6. 闪通臂接扳拦捶

手分解动作

(1) 右手向右划弧,左手向右摆动至头左侧,右手继续向下向左划弧,在腹前屈臂握拳,拳心向下;左手掌心向外,眼平视前方。(图 80、81)

图 80　Fig 80

图 81　Fig 81

(2) 右拳经胸前向体前翻转扳压,肘部微屈,拳心向上,高与胸平;左手经右前臂外侧下落按于左胯旁,手心向下,指尖朝前,眼看右手。

(3) 右拳内旋向右划弧至体前,拳心转向下;右拳继续外旋收至右腰间,拳心转向上;右拳一边内旋一边向前打出,拳心向左高与胸平,肘部微屈。

weight to the left leg. The right heel leaves the ground first. Continue to turn the body to the left until the weight is completely shifted to the left leg. Raise the front part of the right sole slowly and gently and draw it to the inner side of the left foot. The foresole touches the ground first, followed by the whole solid sole. The toes and the knee face to each other. Keep the legs bent. The distance between the feet is 10 – 20cm.

Coordination of the hands and the legs

(1) As the left hand turns over, raise the foot.

(2) As the right hand turns over, draw the foot.

(3) When curving the arms, do not stretch them.

(4) The traverse steps should be done in parallel. While making the steps, be gentle and slow in raising and falling, with only one "point" of the feet touching the ground. Make the feet "empty" or "solid" clearly. While making the feet closer to each other, slightly turn the knees inward. But the feet should not be pigeon-toed, nor should the toes point outward.

6. "Flashing Arm", Followed by "Deflecting Downward, Parrying and Punching"

Illustrations of the hand movements

(1) Swing the right hand to the right along a curved line. Move the left hand to the right and stop at the left side of the head. Continue to move the right hand downward to the left. Bend the arm and form a fist in front of the abdomen, with the centre of the fist facing downward and the left palm facing outward. Remember to look forward. (Fig.80 & 81)

(2) Move the right fist forward past the chest and, while turning it over, press downward. Bend the elbow slightly and the centre of the fist should face upward at chest level. Move the left arm, past the outer side of the right forearm. Fall and press at the side of the left hip, the palm facing down, the fingers pointing forward and the eyes fixed on the right hand.

(4) 左拳经体侧向后向体前拦出，手心斜向上，边外旋边继续向体前拦，手心向右，左手微收附于右前臂内侧，手心向右，指尖斜向上。

脚分解动作

(1) 重心后移，右腿屈坐，左脚尖内扣，身体右转；重心后移，右脚跟离地并以右脚前掌为轴微向内转；上体向右转至面向前方，同时右脚提起收回后不点地即向前迈出，脚跟着地，随即全脚掌踏实，重心在左腿。

(2) 上体微向右转，右脚尖外撇，右腿屈膝，重心前移至右腿，随转体左退屈膝，左脚跟离地，左脚向前迈出，脚跟着地，两脚脚跟横向距离不超过 10 公分；身体重心前移，左膝屈弓，右腿自然伸直成左弓步，上体正直，松腰松胯。

手脚配合

(1) 转体扣脚，摆臂划弧，重心左移，握拳收脚。(图 82)

图 82　Fig 82

(3) Twist the right fist inward and curve it to the right and stop in front of the body. Turn over the centre of the fist and continue to twist the fist outward. Draw it to the right side of the waist with the centre of the fist upward. Punch the right fist forward while turning it inward. The centre of the fist should face the left at chest level with the elbow slightly bent.

(4) Move the left fist from behind past the side of the body, parry forward with the palm slanting upward. With the outward-turning of the hand, continue to parry forward. The palm should face the right. Slightly draw the left hand to the inner side of the right forearm, with the palm facing the right and the fingers slanting upward.

Illustrations of the leg movements

(1) Move the weight backward, bend and squat on the right leg as the left toes turn inward. Turn the body to the right. Continue to move the weight backward. Lift the right heel and, with the right foresole as an axis, slightly turn the right foot inward. Continue turning the body to the right until one faces forward. Meanwhile, lift the right foot, draw it back, but do not touch the ground. Then immediately step forward, the heel on the ground first, then make a solid whole sole. At this moment, the weight is on the left leg.

(2) Slightly turn the body to the right with the right toes pointing outward. Bend the right leg and move the weight forward to the right leg as the body turns. Bend the left knee and lift the left heel. Step forward with the left leg, with the heel on the ground. The parallel distance between the two heels should be no more than 10cm. Move the weight forward and bend the left knee like a bow. Stretch the right leg naturally to form a left bow step. The body at this time should be erect and the waist and hips should be loose.

Coordination of the hands and the legs

(1) Turn the body and the foot inward. Swing the right arm along a curved line, shift the weight to the left, make a fist with the right hand and draw back the foot. (Fig.82)

(2) 摆步扳拳。(图 83)

(3) 转体旋臂。(图 84)

(4) 上步拦掌。(图 85)

(5) 弓步打拳。(图 86)

图 83　Fig 83

图 84　Fig 84

图 85　Fig 85

三、24 式太极拳动作说明和练习要点

预备式

身体自然直立,两脚并拢,脚尖向前,两腿自然伸直;胸腹自然放松,两臂下垂,手指微屈,两手垂于大腿外侧,头颈正直,下颏回收,口闭齿扣,舌抵上腭;精神集中,表情自然,双眼平视前方。(图 87)

(2) Step forward and deflect the fist. (Fig. 83)

(3) Turn the body and twist the arm. (Fig. 84)

(4) Step forward and parry with the palm. (Fig. 85)

(5) Make a bow step and punch with the fist. (Fig. 86)

图 86　　Fig 86

Ⅲ. Illustrations and Instructions of the Movements of 24 – Form *Taijiquan*

Preparation

图 87　　Fig 87

Stand naturally with the feet close and pointing forward and the two legs straightened up naturally. Both the chest and the abdomen relax with the arms and hands hanging naturally at the sides. Bend the fingers slightly. Hold the head and the neck erect with the chin drawn slightly inward. Close the mouth and bite the teeth with the tongue tip resting on the hard palate. Concentrate with a natural expression on the face and the eyes looking forward. (Fig. 87)

1. 起势

图 88　　Fig 88

(1) 左腿开立：左脚向左分开一步，两脚平行同肩宽，成开立步。(图 88)

(2) 两臂前举：两臂慢慢向前平举，与肩同宽，两臂自然伸直，肘关节微屈，两手心向下，指尖向前。(图 89)

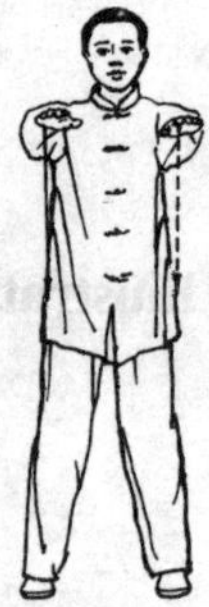

图 89　　Fig 89

(3) 屈腿按掌：两腿慢慢屈膝半蹲，重心平均落在两腿之间，两掌按至腹前，上体正直，如端坐在椅子上，两眼平视前方。(图 90)

练习要点

(1) 由并步站立变为开立步时，应能使左膝放松，重心移至右腿，左腿放松而后轻轻提起左脚跟，随之前脚掌离地，以不超过右踝的高度向左分开半步；落脚时左前脚掌先着地，随之全脚掌着地。上述重心的转移虽然简单，但体现了太极拳运动“轻起轻落，点起点落”这一重要的步法规律。

(2) 手臂前举时，两手先在两腿外侧将掌心转至身体的后方向，随即慢慢地向体前平举，好像要把一根下端踩在脚下、上端系于手腕的橡皮筋拉长扯起来，既要有一定紧张度，又不松懈。不要出现指尖朝下的“折腕”错误动作。

1. Commencing Movement

(1) The left leg steps apart

The left foot steps half-step left, and stand naturally with the feet shoulder-width apart. (Fig.88)

(2) Raise the arms forward

Raise the arms slowly forward and upward to shoulder level with shoulder width. Straighten the arms forward naturally with the palms facing downward and the fingers pointing forward. The elbows drop towards the knees. (Fig.89)

(3) Bend the knees with the palms pressing down gently

Bend the knees while distributing the weight equally on both legs. Press the palms down gently in front of the abdomen. Keep the torso erect as if sitting on a chair and look forward. (Fig.90)

图 90　　Fig 90

Points to remember

(1) When step left apart, relax the left knee, then shift the weight onto the right leg. Keep the left leg relaxed. Raise the left heel gently then the whole left sole not higher over the right malleolus. Load the front part of the left sole first on the ground and then the whole sole. Shifting weight seems simple but it indicates one of the important regulations in practising *taijiquan* —"gently raise and gently down, gently put toes on or off the ground."

（3）屈膝下蹲的高度要视练习者的身体素质而定并因人而异，不要一刀切。在24式太极拳演练过程中，除少数姿势外，整套拳术都在半蹲的状态中进行。开始的屈膝高度基本上就是整套拳的高度，练习中不可忽高忽低。

易犯错误

（1）向左迈步时，身体左右摇晃。

（2）两臂前举和下按时，两肘尖外撑、上扬，两肩上耸。

（3）下蹲时，身体前俯后仰。

（4）两臂前举和两掌下按时，腕关节过于松软，造成指尖朝下的“折腕”或指尖朝上的“翘手指”的错误动作。

2. 野马分鬃

1）左野马分鬃

图 91　　**Fig 91**

（1）收脚抱球：上体稍向右转，右臂屈抱于右胸前，手高不过肩，肘略低于手腕，右手心向下，左手外旋手心向上，左臂屈抱于腹前，两手上下相对，如在右肋前抱球，左脚收至右脚内侧，脚尖点地，眼看右手。（图91）

(2) Turn the palms toward the back first, then raise the arms up gently. The arms and hands should be neither too tense nor too loose. The fingers should not be bent downward.

(3) One decides by him/herself how much s/he can bend the knees down. In exercising the 24-Form *taijiquan* one has to bend the knees most of the time except for a few movements. When one bends his or her knees to a certain height at the very beginning, s/he should keep the same height through the whole exercise.

Wrong movements

(1) Keep moving the torso right and left when step left apart.

(2) While raising the arms forward or downward, point the elbows outward or upward, and hold the shoulders upward.

(3) While bending the knees, the torso moves forward or backward.

(4) The wrists are too loose so that the fingertips point down while raising the arms and the fingertips point up while pressing the palms downward.

2. Parting a Wild Horse's Mane on Both Sides

1) Parting a Wild Horse's Mane on the Left Side

(1) Hold the hands and draw the foot inside

Turn the torso slightly to the right and raise the right hand not higher than the shoulder level until the forearm is horizontal in front of the right chest. Drop the right elbow a bit lower than the right wrist and the right palm faces down; meanwhile the left hand moves in an outward arc and the left palm faces upward. Keep moving the left forearm horizontally in front of the abdomen until it comes under the right hand, the palms facing each other as if holding a ball. Move the left foot beside the right foot, with the toes on the floor. Look at the right hand. (Fig. 91)

(2) 转体上步:上体左转,左脚向左前方迈出一步,脚跟轻轻着地,重心仍在右腿。(图 92)

图 92 Fig 92

图 93 Fig 93

(3) 弓步分手:上体继续左转,重心前移,左脚踏实,左腿屈膝前弓;右腿自然蹬直,右脚跟外展成左弓步;两掌前后分开,左手分至体前,高与眼平,手心斜向上,右手按至右胯旁,手心向下,指尖向前,两臂稍屈,眼看左手。(图 93)

2) 右野马分鬃

图 94 Fig 94

(1) 转体撇脚:重心稍向后移,左脚尖翘起外撇,上体稍左转,两手翻转准备"抱球",眼看左手。(图 94)

(2) Turn the body and step forward

Turn the body to the left as the left foot steps leftward. Rest the left heel gently on the ground. The weight remains on the right leg. (Fig.92)

(3) "Bow step" and hands apart

Keep moving the body to the left. Shift the weight forward and rest the left foot on the ground. Bend the left knee forward. Straighten the right leg with the heel pressing down on the floor to form a left "bow step". As one turns the body slightly leftward, gradually raise the left forearm obliquely to eye level with the palm facing upward and the elbow slightly bent and the lower right hand beside the right hip with the palm facing downward and the fingers pointing forward. Look at the left hand. (Fig.93)

2) Parting a Wild Horse's Mane on the Right Side

(1) Turn the body and point the toes outward

Shift the weight backward. Raise the toes of the left foot slightly and outward. Turn the body slightly to the left and the two hands are ready to make a "ball-holding" gesture. Look at the right hand. (Fig.94)

(2) 抱手收脚：上体继续左转左手，翻转成手心向下在左胸前屈抱，腕同肩高，肘略低于腕；右手翻转前摆，手心向上，在腹前屈抱，两手上下相对，在左肋前成抱球状；重心转至左脚，左脚踏实，右脚收至左脚内侧，脚尖点地；眼看左手。(图 95、96)

图 95　　Fig 95

图 96　　Fig 96

图 97　　Fig 97

(3) 转体上步：上体稍右转，右脚向右前方迈出一步，脚跟轻轻着地。(图 97)

(4) 弓步分手：上体继续右转，重心前移，右脚踏实，右腿屈膝前弓，左腿自然蹬直，左脚跟外展成右弓步；两手前后分开，右手分至体前，高与眼平，手心斜向上，左手按至左胯旁，手心向下，指尖向前，两臂微屈，眼看右手。(图 98)

(2) Hold the hands and draw the foot back

Keep turning the torso to the left. Turn the left palm downward in front of the left chest with the wrist at the shoulder level and the elbow lower than the wrist. Turn the right hand with the palm facing upward and the palms facing each other as if holding a ball in front of the left chest. Shift the weight onto the left foot, then draw the right foot forward beside the left foot and rest the toes on the floor. Look at the left hand. (Fig.95 & 96)

(3) Turn the body and step forward

Turn the torso slightly to the right, and move the right foot a step rightward with the heel pressing gently on the floor. (Fig.97)

(4) Bow step with the hands apart

Keep turning the torso to the right and shift the weight forward to press the right foot on the floor. Straighten the left leg with the heel outward pressing down on the floor to make a right bow step. At the same time gradually raise the right hand obliquely upward higher to eye level with the palm facing obliquely upward and the elbow slightly bent, and press the left hand down beside the left hip with the palm facing downward and the fingers pointing forward. Look at the right hand. (Fig.98)

图 98 **Fig** 98

3）左野马分鬃

(1) 转体撇脚：重心后移，右脚尖翘起外撇，上体稍右转，两手翻转准备"抱球"。（图 99）

图 99　Fig 99

图 100　Fig 100

(2) 抱手收脚：上体继续右转，右手翻转在右胸前屈抱，左手前摆翻转，在腹前屈抱，两手上下相对，好像在右肋前抱球；重心前移，右脚踏实，左脚收至右脚内侧，脚尖点地；眼看右手。（图 100）

(3) 转体上步，同前。（图 101）

(4) 弓步分手，同前。（图 102）

攻防含义

野马分鬃的手法是下采、前靠。例如，对方右手打来，我右手擒住对方手腕向下采引，同时左脚上步落在对方身右外侧，左前臂随之插入对方右腋下，用转腰分靠之力使对方仰倒。

3) Parting a Wild Horse's Mane on the Left Side

(1) Turn the body and point the toes outward

Shift the weight a bit backward. Raise the toes of the right foot and point them outward, turn the torso slightly to the right, and the two hands are ready to make a "ball-holding" gesture. (Fig. 99)

(2) Hold hands and draw the foot back

Keep turning the torso to the right. Turn the right palm downward and turn the left hand with the palm facing upward so that the palms face each other as if holding a ball in front of the right chest. Raise the right foot and press it on the floor while shifting the weight forward. Then draw the left foot forward beside the right foot and rest the toes on the floor. Look at the right hand. (Fig. 100)

(3) Turn the body and step forward.

Repeat movement in 1): (2). (Fig. 101)

(4) Bow step with the hands apart

Repeat movement in 1): (3). (Fig. 102)

图 101 **Fig 101**

图 102 **Fig 102**

The meaning of attack and defence

The movements of the hands in Parting a Wild Horse's Mane on Both Sides are to press downward and ram forward. For example: When the opponent hits you with his/her right hand, hold his/her right

练习要点

(1) 左右野马分鬃,抱球时不能像做体操那样肘弯夹紧,手、臂、肘都与肩平;应使肩部放松,腕部稍弯,手指微屈,肘低于肩,腕与肩高,腕低于手;屈肘时,前臂与大臂之间的夹角应大於90°,手腕、前臂同胸部之间应有20至30厘米的距离,整个上方的手臂成弧形。

(2) 如"左脚收至右脚内侧,脚尖点地",这时绝大部分体重落在右腿上,左脚尖点地只起到一点辅助支撑的作用,待动作熟练以后,左脚收向右脚内侧足弓附近即可,脚尖不点地。以后类似的过渡动作,均应照此理解。这里的脚尖点地是指用脚前掌着地。

(3) 假如起势时面向南,起步时先转体至面向南偏东,弓步完成时再转体面向正东。在连续练习时,这两次转体要一气呵成,不可间断。

(4) 弓步时两脚跟之间有20至30厘米横向的宽度。前脚的脚尖朝正前方,后脚脚尖与正前方成一定的角度。前弓腿的膝关节和脚尖在一条垂直线上。

(5) 眼神是太极拳运动的一个重要部分。一般规律是视线随主要动作的手移动,保持头颈正直,目光平视。要避免低头或歪头,也不要死盯着前手,那样反而紧张呆滞。应把视线不时平移远望,有张有弛。

wrist with your right hand and press it downward. At the same time, kick his/her right side with your left foot and insert your left forearm in his/her right armpit. Turn your waist and make an effort to lay him/her on the ground.

Points to remember

(1) Do not bend the elbow too tight and do not keep the hands, arms and elbows all at the same level of the shoulders. Drop the shoulders loose and bend the fingers a little bit. Put the elbows lower than the shoulders and the wrists lower than the hands to keep the same level of the shoulders. While bending the elbows, form a 90-degree angle between the forearms and the upper arms. Keep the two arms a distance of about 20 – 30cm to the chest.

(2) When "draw the left/right foot forward beside the right/left foot and rest the toes on the floor", most of the weight is on the right/left foot. Resting the toes on the floor just functions as a supporter. When you become a master, just draw one foot beside the other without resting the toes on the floor. Whenever you make this movement, do like this. Resting the toes on the floor means pressing the front part of the sole on the floor.

(3) If you face south to commence the movements, when you turn the body and step forward, you should face southeast. And When you form the "bow step", you should face east. The two torso-turning movements should be done smoothly without a break in between.

(4) When you form a "bow step", you should keep a parallel distance of 20 – 30cm between the two heels. The front foot should point straight forward while the hind foot should not. The front knee and toes should be on a vertical line.

(5) Eye movement is a very important part in *taijiquan*. Usually look at the hand which makes the main movements and hold the head and neck erect. The sight should be straight forward. Do not drop the

3. 白鹤亮翅

(1) 跟步抱球：上体稍左转，右腿向前跟步，前脚掌轻轻落于左脚后；两手翻转相对，在胸前屈臂“抱球”，左手在上右手在下，眼看左手。（图 103、104）

图 103　Fig 103

图 104　Fig 104

(2) 后坐转体：重心换至右脚，右脚踏实，上体后坐并稍向右转体；两手开始交错分开，右手向右上举，左手下落；眼看右手。（图 105、106）

图 105　Fig 105

图 106　Fig 106

(3) 虚步分手：左脚稍前移，脚前掌着地成左虚步；右手分至右额前，掌心向内，左手按左胯旁；眼平视前方。（图 107、108）

head down or push the head aside. Nor should you fix the sight on the front hand to make the movement and expression stiff. Shift the eyesight straight back and forth.

3. A White Crane Spreading Its Wings

(1) Step forward to "hold a ball"

Turn the torso slightly to the left. Step the right foot a half step forward and rest the front sole lightly behind the left foot. Turn the two palms to face each other to make a ball-holding gesture in front of the left chest with the left hand on top. Look at the left hand. (Fig. 103 & 104)

(2) "Sit back" and turn the torso

Shift the weight onto the right foot, sit back and turn the torso slightly to the right. The two hands cross and then part with the right hand up and the left down, the eyes looking at the right hand. (Fig. 105 & 106)

(3) "Weak step" and hands apart

Move the left foot slightly forward and rest the toes lightly on the floor to make a left "weak step". At the same time raise the right hand beside the right temple, with the palm turning inward, while the left hand moves downward beside the left hip, with the palm turning downward. Look straight ahead. (Fig. 107 & 108)

图 107 Fig 107

图 108 Fig 108

攻防含义

白鹤亮翅的攻防含义有二。一是对方双掌向我攻来,我急用两手上下分开对方两掌,瓦解其攻势。二是对方右手攻来,我用左手擒住其右腕,右臂插入对方右腋下,用转腰横挒之力使其前扑。

练习要点

(1) 本势的步型是虚步,步法是跟步。虚步应做到上体松正,两腿虚实分明,重心稳定。跟步时,应先向前移重心,右脚轻轻提起,随之全脚掌逐渐离地,缓慢地前跟半步,然后右脚掌轻轻落地,重心慢慢后移,右脚逐渐踏实。右脚由虚变实,支撑大部分体重,最后将左脚轻轻地前移,由实变虚,调整成左脚前脚掌着地的左虚步。

(2) 做此势练习时,必须注意在腰部的旋转带动下协调运动。即右脚前跟步时腰部左转,身体后坐时腰部微右转,最后调整步型时身体再转向正前方。

易犯错误

(1) 虚步时出现上体后仰,挺髋挺腹;上体前俯,挺胸突臀;两脚横向距离过小或过大;两腿虚实不明,体重落于两腿之间。

(2) 两臂外撑不够,肘部过于弯曲,右臂大、小臂的夹角小于90°。

The meaning of attack and defence

When the opponent attacks with both palms, use your hands to beat them apart to crumble their force. When the opponent attacks with his/her right hand, use your left hand to hold his/her right wrist and, at the same time, insert your right arm into the opponent's right armpit. Then turn your waist to push the opponent forward face down to the ground.

Points to remember

(1) The steps in this section are "weak" steps. By "weak" step, it means to keep the torso relaxed and make one leg "weak" and the other "strong" so as to keep the weight in the right position. When move the step forward, shift the weight forward; then raise the right foot gently and move forward slowly. Afterwards, rest the right sole on the floor, the right foot becoming "strong" and bearing most of the weight while the left foot moving forward a little and becoming "weak" to make a weak step.

(2) When turn the waist, pay attention to the coordination of the movements. That is to say: turn the waist slight to the left while moving the right foot forward; when sit back, turn the waist slightly to the right; and turn the torso straight forward when coordinate the step at the end.

Wrong movements

(1) When make a "weak" step, either thrust the torso backward or the chest forward. The knee is not bent to make a "weak" step while the other knee turns inward. The two feet is either too wide apart or too close together. Shift the weight neither on the right leg nor on the left leg, but just between the two legs, making it hard to tell which is a "weak" step.

(2) The two hands do not stretch outward thoroughly. The elbows are over bent to make an angle under 90 degrees between the upper arms and the forearms.

4. 搂膝拗步

1）左搂膝拗步

(1) 转体掩臂：身体左转，右手向左摆至体前，手心转向斜上；眼看右手。（图 109、110）

图 109 **Fig 109**

图 110 **Fig 110**

(2) 掩臂收脚：上体右转，右手自体前下落，经右胯侧向右后方上举，与头同高，手心向上；左手同时自左侧上举经头前向右划弧落至右肩前，手心向下，同时左脚收右脚内侧，脚尖点地；头随手转，眼看右手。（图 111）

(3) 上步屈肘：上体稍左转，左脚向左前方迈出一步，脚跟轻轻落地；右臂屈肘，右手收至右肩上，虎口对耳，掌心斜向下；左手落至右腹前；眼看前方。（图 112）

4. Brushing the Knees and Twisting the Steps on Both Sides

1) Brushing the Left Knee and Twist the Step on the Left Side

(1) Turn the torso and cover up the arms

Turn the body to the left, move the right hand to the front of the chest with the palm facing obliquely upward. Look at the right hand. (Fig.109 & 110)

(2) Cover up the arm and draw the foot forward

Turn the torso to the right, move the right hand downward past the right hip and up back to the right to head level with the palm facing upward. Meanwhile, move the left hand, first in an upward, then in a downward curve, stopping before the right shoulder, the palm facing down. At the same time move the left foot to the right foot with the toes on the floor. The head follows the right hand and the eyes also look at it. (Fig.111)

(3) Step forward and bend the elbow

Turn the torso slightly to the left. Step the left foot forward with the heel on the ground. Bend the right elbow and at the same time draw the right hand up to the shoulder, then to the head at the ear level with the palm facing obliquely downward. Draw the left hand to the right abdomen and look forward. (Fig.112)

图 111 **Fig 111**

图 112 **Fig 112**

(4) 弓步搂推：上体继续左转，重心前移，左脚踏实，左腿屈弓，右脚自然蹬直成左弓步；左手经左膝前上方搂过，停于左胯旁，掌心向下，指尖向前；右手向前推出，与鼻尖相对，掌心向前，指尖向上，右臂自然伸直，肘微屈垂。眼看右手。(图 113)

图 113 **Fig 113**

图 114 **Fig 114**

2) 右搂膝拗步

(1) 转体撇脚：重心后移，左脚尖翘起外撇；上体左转，两臂外旋开始摆动；眼看右手。(图 114)

(2) 摆臂收脚：上体继续左转，重心前移，左脚踏实，右脚收至左脚内侧，脚尖点地；右手经头前划弧摆至左肩前，掌心向下，左手向左上前划弧上举，摆至与肩同高，掌心向上；眼看左手。(图 115、116)

(4) "Bow step" and brush and twist

Keep turning the torso to the left. Shift the weight forward. Place the left foot flat on the floor. Then bend the left leg and straighten the right leg to make a "bow step". Drop the left hand to circle the left knee and stop beside the left hip with the palm facing downward and the finger tips forward. Push the right hand forward at nose level with the palm facing forward and the finger tips upward. Straighten the right arm naturally with the elbow slightly bent. Look at the right hand. (Fig. 113)

2) Brushing the Right Knee and Twisting the Step on the Right Side

(1) Turn the body with the toes up

Shift the weight backward. Raise the toes of the left foot slightly and turn the toes outward. Turn the torso to the left with the two arms making an arc. Look at the right hand. (Fig. 114)

(2) Move the arms and draw the foot forward

Keep turning the torso to the left. Shift the weight forward. Push the left foot flat on the floor. Draw the right foot to the left foot with the toes on the floor. The right hand, passing front of the head, make an arc pausing in front of the left shoulder, palm facing downward. At the same time turn the left hand up leftward to make an arc, pausing at the shoulder level, palm facing upward. Look at the left hand. (Fig. 115 & 116)

图 115　**Fig** 115

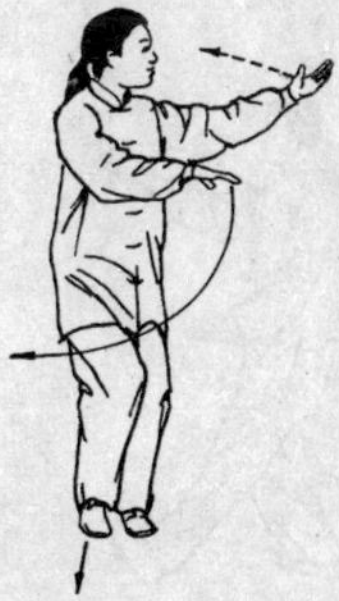

图 116　**Fig** 116

(3) 上步屈肘:上体稍右转;右脚向右前方迈出一步,脚跟轻轻落地;左臂屈肘左手收左肩上,虎口与耳相对,掌心斜向前,右手落至左腹前。眼看前方。(图 117、118)

(4) 弓步搂推:上体继续右转,重心前移,右脚踏实,右腿屈弓,左腿自然伸直成左弓步;右手经右膝前上方搂过停于右腿外,掌心向下,指尖向前;左手向前推出,与鼻尖相对,掌心向前,指尖向上,左臂自然弯曲,肘微屈垂。眼看左手。(图 119)

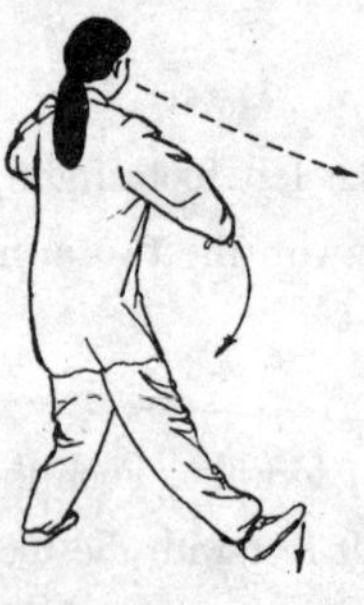
图 117 **Fig 117**

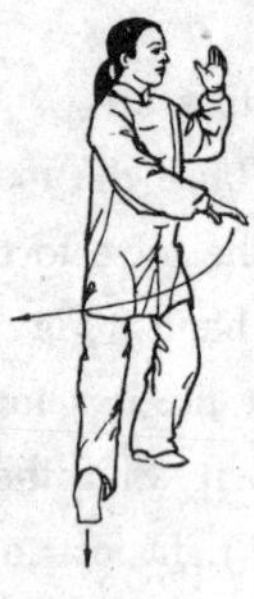
图 118 **Fig 118**

图 119 **Fig 119**

3) 左搂膝拗步

动作与右搂膝拗步相同,只是左右方向相反。(图 120 ~ 123)

图 120 **Fig 120**

图 121 **Fig 121**

(3) Draw the step forward and bend the elbow

Turn the torso slightly to the right. Move the right foot a step forward with the heel lightly on the floor. Bend the left elbow and move the left hand sideways up to shoulder level, then to the head at ear level, with the palm facing obliquely forward while the right hand moves to the front of the left abdomen. Look forward. (Fig. 117 & 118)

(4) "Bow step" and brush and twist

Keep turning the torso to the right. Shift the weight forward and place the right foot flat on the floor. Bend the right knee slightly and straighten the left leg naturally to make a "bow step". Drop the right hand to circle the right knee and stop beside the right hip with the palm facing downward and the finger tips forward. Push the left hand forward to the nose level with the palm facing forward and the finger tips upward. Stretch the left arm naturally and bend the elbow slightly. Look at the left hand. (Fig.119)

3) Brushing the Left Knee and Twisting the Step on the Left Side

The movements in this section are the same as the movements in "Brushing the right knee and twisting the step on the right side", except in the opposite direction. (Fig.120 – 123)

图 122 **Fig** 122

图 123 **Fig** 123

攻防含义

一手搂对方攻来的手脚，另一只手向前推打反击。

练习要点

(1) 搂膝拗步与野马分鬃同是连续向前的三个弓步，所不同的是本势是手脚左右异侧的拗弓步。为了保证重心的稳定，两脚左右的宽度一定要保持在20～30厘米左右，切忌两脚踩在一条直线上或左右交叉，防止上体歪扭。

(2) 在上步过程中，后脚收至支撑脚内侧，脚尖点地，这是为了照顾初学者支撑无力、重心掌握不稳的困难。一旦动作熟练后，应逐步取消脚尖点地，使后脚经支撑脚内侧时不停不落，连续稳定地向前迈出。对控制能力较强的初学者完全可以直接连续上步，不必点地支撑。

(3) 本势的手法是以"搂""推"为主。搂掌的动作较简单。以左掌为例，左掌以右肩前向下落划弧经膝前搂到左腿侧，到体侧时要坐腕、展掌、舒指。初学者的推掌(以右掌为例)，右掌从右侧后上方先屈肘，使掌收到耳侧，虎口对耳，此时手掌和手腕部都要放松，体现由实到虚的变化，当推到顶点时，"虚"掌变"实"掌。舒指、展掌、虎口撑圆、掌根前顶，腕肘下沉。前推、下搂的两掌要和弓步同时到位，上下相随。

易犯错误

(1) 弓步左右横向距离过大过小，上体歪斜，重心不稳。

The meaning of attack and defence

When your opponent attacks you with his/her hands and feet, brush his/her hands and feet away with one hand and push him/her with the other hand.

Points to remember

(1) The three "bow steps" in "Parting a Wild Horse's Mane on Both Sides" are different from the three "bow steps" in "Brushing the Knees and Twisting the Steps on Both Sides". To make the "bow steps" in "Brushing the Knees and Twisting the Steps on Both Sides" is to brush the knees and twist the steps. To coordinate the palm, waist and leg movements the distance between the two heels should be between 20cm and 30cm. To keep the torso erect, do not twist the two feet or put one foot behind the other on the same line.

(2) When drawing the foot forward, resting the toes on the floor is a good way to help beginners to keep balance. When one becomes more skillful, she/he does not need to rest the toes on the floor to keep balance. Instead one just raises the toes and turns them slightly outward before placing the foot flat on the floor.

(3) The essential hand techniques of this movement are the "brushing" and "pushing". The "brushing" is relatively simple. Take the movement of the left hand for example. The left hand should move downward along a curved route from the right shoulder, brush the left knee and then stop at the outer side of the left leg, where you should sit the wrist a bit and stretch the palm and fingers. In "pushing", take the right hand for instance, first bend the right arm with the palm at ear level, the fingerpit facing the ear, and the palm and wrist relaxed. When the hand pushes forward to its ultimate, the relaxed palm should take on some strength, the fingers, palm and fingerpit should be stretched, the lower part of the palm should push forward, and the wrist and elbow should be lowered a bit. The pushing, brushing and palm-stretching should coordinate and be simultaneous with the bow step.

(2) 摆臂时腰部不转动，单纯地抡臂。

(3)“搂”“推”的手臂过于紧张，推掌过直过远。搂手不是搂膝而是搂腹。屈肘后拉，造成肩、臂紧张，上体前俯。

5. 手挥琵琶

(1) 跟步伸臂：右腿向前收半步，前脚掌轻落于左脚后与左脚跟相距约一脚长；右臂稍向前伸展，腕关节放松。（图 124）

(2) 后坐引手：重心后移，右脚踏实，左手向左向上划弧摆至体前，手臂自然伸直，掌心斜向下；右手屈臂后引，收到胸前，掌心斜向下，眼转至看左手。（图 125）

(3) 虚步合手：上体稍向左回转，左脚稍向前移，脚跟着地成左虚步；两臂外旋，屈肘合把，两手前后交错，侧掌合于体前。左手与鼻相对，掌心向右；右手与左肘相对，右掌心向左。眼看左手。（图 126）

图 124　Fig 124

图 125　Fig 125

图 126　Fig 126

Wrong movements

(1) While making a bow step, the parallel distance between the two heels is either too wide or too narrow. In this case it is hard to keep the torso erect and one loses balance easily.

(2) When the arms are making arcs, the waist is stiff.

(3) The arms are stiff while pushing forward. Brush the abdomen instead of the knee. Drawing the bent elbow back makes the arm and shoulder stiff and the torso forward.

5. Playing the Lute

(1) Move the foot forward and straighten the arms

Move the right foot a half step forward and place the front sole lightly on the floor behind the left heel. The distance between the left heel and the right toes is one foot. Move the arm slightly forward with the wrist relaxed. (Fig. 124)

(2) Sit back and raise the hands

Shift the weight back and place the right foot flat on the floor. Meanwhile, raise the left hand leftward in a curve to the front of the chest and the arm straightens naturally with the palm facing obliquely downward. Bend the right arm and draw it backward to the front of the chest with the palm facing obliquely downward. Look at the left hand. (Fig. 125)

(3) "Weak step" and the hands meet

Turn the torso slightly back to the left, raise the left foot and place it slightly forward, the heel coming down on the floor and the knee bent a bit to form a left "weak step". Raise both arms in a curve, the elbows slightly bent. Move the two hands crisscross and meet in the front. Raise the left hand to nose level with the palm facing right. Move the right hand downward until it reaches the inner side of the left elbow with the right palm facing left. Look at the left hand. (Fig. 126)

攻防含义

手法是合手撅臂。当对方右手打来，我用右手握其腕部，顺势向后牵引，同时左手贴于对方肘关节处，然后两手左右用力内合，采用反关节擒拿方法，使对方右臂伤折。

练习要点

(1) 后坐引手时，前臂和右手引带的动作是在上体后坐并右转、重心后移、右脚逐渐踏实的过程中协调一致地同时进行的。身法、手法和步法协调配合防止动作生硬僵化。

(2) 定势时，两臂应半屈成弧形，舒展圆满。肘部不要过分弯屈，两臂紧缩，夹肘夹腋，动作僵直。

(3) 虚步时不要俯身突臀或仰身挺腹。

6. 倒卷肱

1) 右倒卷肱

图 127　　**Fig** 127

(1) 转身撤手：上体稍右转，两手翻转向上，右手向下经腰两侧向右肩划弧上举与肩同高，左手前伸停于体前，头随右手转至右后，眼看右手。(图 127)

(2) 退步卷肱：上体稍左转，左脚提起后退一步，脚前掌轻轻落地；右臂屈肘卷肱，右手收至肩上，经耳侧再前推，掌心斜向前下方，左手开始回收；眼看左手。(图 128)

图 128　　**Fig** 128

The meaning of attack and defence

When the opponent attacks with his/her right hand, you use you right hand to hold the opponent's wrist and draw him/her back. Meanwhile, place your left hand on his/her elbow and then push both your hands together to break his/her right arm.

Points to remember

(1) When you draw the opponent back, sit back and turn right. Shift the weight backward and place the right foot gradually flat on the floor. Coordinate the weight transfer with the hand and foot movements.

(2) Don't over bend the elbows or press both arms on both sides.

(3) When making a "weak" step, the torso should be kept erect.

6. Stepping Back and Whirling the Arms on Both Sides

1) Stepping back and Whirling the Arm on the Right Side

(1) Turn the torso and draw the hand back

Turn the torso to the right and turn both hands up. Then move the right hand downward past the side of the waist to draw an arc up right backward to the level of the shoulder. Stretch the left hand forward and stop in the front. The head follows the right hand to turn to the back right. Look at the right hand. (Fig. 127)

(2) Step back and bend the arm

Turn the torso slightly to the left, raise the left foot and step back with the front sole placed flat on the floor lightly. Bend the right arm and draw the right hand past the ear before pushing it obliquely ahead with the palm facing obliquely forward, and start to pull the left hand back. Look at the left hand. (Fig. 128)

图 129　　Fig 129

(3) 虚步推手：上体继续左转，重心后移，左脚踏实，右脚以脚掌为轴将脚调正，脚跟离地，右膝微屈成右虚步；右手推至体前，掌心向前，腕与肩平，左手回收至左腰间；眼看右手。(图 129)

2) 左倒卷肱

(1) 转体撤手：上体稍左转，右手翻转向上，左手向左后方划弧上举，与头同高，掌心向上。头随体转，眼看左手。(图 130)

(2) 退步卷肱：上体稍右转，右脚提起向后退一步，前脚掌轻轻落地；左臂屈肘卷收，左手收至肩上经耳侧前推，掌心斜向前下方，右手开始后收；眼看右手。(图 131)

(3) 虚步推掌：上体继续右转，重心后移，右脚踏实，左脚以前脚掌为轴将脚调正，脚跟离地，左膝微屈成左虚步；左手推至体前，腕与肩平，掌心向前，右手向后回收至右腰间；眼看左手。(图 132)

图 130　　Fig 130

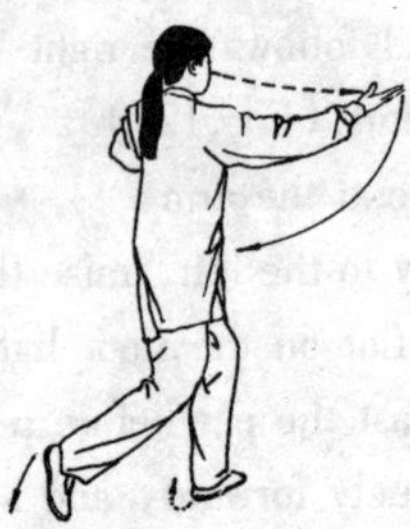

图 131　　Fig 131

图 132　　Fig 132

(3) "Weak step" and push the palm forward

Keep turning the torso to the left. Shift the weight backward and place the left foot flat on the floor. Pivot on the right front sole until the right foot comes in line with the body. Raise the heel first and bend the right knee to make a right "weak step". Push the right hand ahead with the palm facing forward and keep the wrist at the same level of the shoulder. Pull the left hand back beside the waist with the palm facing upward. Look at the right hand. (Fig. 129)

2) Stepping Back and Whirling the Arm on the Left Side

(1) Turn the torso and draw the hand back

Turn the torso to the left. Move the right hand up. The left hand draws an arc up left backward to the level of the head with the palm facing upward. The head follows the body to turn. Look at the left hand. (Fig. 130)

(2) Step back and bend the arm

Turn the torso slightly to the right, raise the right foot and step back with the front sole placed flat on the floor lightly. Bend the left arm and draw the left hand past the ear, then push it ahead with the palm facing obliquely downward. Start to pull the right hand back and look at the right hand. (Fig. 131)

(3) "Weak step" and push the palm forward

Keep turning the torso to the right. Shift the weight backward and place the right foot flat on the floor. Pivot on the left front sole until the left foot comes in line with the body. Raise the heel first and bend the left knee to make a left "weak step". Push the left hand ahead with the palm facing forward and keep the wrist at the same level of the shoulder. Pull the right hand back beside the waist with the palm facing upward. Look at the left hand. (Fig. 132)

3) 右倒卷肱:同 1)(图 133~135)

图 133　Fig 133

图 134　Fig 134

图 135　Fig 135

4) 左倒卷肱;同 2)(图 136~138)

攻防含义

在退守中反击。当对方右手攻来,我用左手接住,顺势退步牵引,右手则突然向前击打对方胸部。

练习要点

(1) 本势的步法是在虚步基础上的连续退步。练习时注意“重心平稳”、“点起点落”、“轻起轻落”的要点。

(2) 退步与卷肱同时完成,后移重心与前推手同时完成,协调一致。

(3) 每个倒卷肱的第三动虚步推手的完成势是本势的定势,动作由虚转为实,微微一沉,然后再接做下一个式子的动作。

(4) 第一动的转体撤手完成势,两臂的打开角度约为 120°至 135°左右为宜。

3) Stepping Back and Whirling the Arm on the Right Side

Repeat the movements in 1). (Fig.133 – 135)

4) Stepping Back and Whirling the Arm on the Left Side

Repeat the movements in 2). (Fig.136 – 138)

图 136 **Fig** 136

图 137 **Fig** 137

图 138 **Fig** 138

The meaning of attack and defence

To attack in defence: When the opponent attacks you with his/her right hand, hold it with your left hand and pull it. At the same time, hit his/her chest with your right hand.

Points to remember

(1) All the "back steps" in this section are based on "weak steps". In doing the "weak steps", remember to keep the balance and put the toes on/off the floor lightly.

(2) Step back and whirl the arm simultaneously. And "sit back" and push the hand simultaneously.

(3) When stepping back, after placing the toes down, setting the whole foot on the floor and whirling the arm, pause a while and then continue the next movement.

(4) While pushing out the hands, the angle made by the hands should be 120 to 135 degrees.

易犯错误

(1) 退步时两脚落在一条直线上或“拧麻花”。

(2) 手慢脚快或手快脚慢都造成上下不协调的错误。

7. 左揽雀尾

(1) 抱手收脚:上体右转,右手自腰间向后向上划弧至右胸前屈臂“抱球”,掌心向下;左手自体前向下向右腹划弧屈抱于腹前,掌心向上,左右手相对成抱球状;左脚收至右脚内侧,脚尖点地;眼看右手。(图 139)

(2) 转体上步:上体左转,左脚向左前方迈出一步,脚跟着地;眼看左手。(图 140)

图 139　Fig 139

图 140　Fig 140

(3) 弓步掤臂:上体继续左转,重心前移,左脚踏实,左膝屈膝前弓,右腿自然蹬直成左弓步;两手前后分开,左前臂屈于胸前掤架,掌心向内,右手向下按于右胯旁,掌心向下,指尖向前;眼看左手。(图 141)

Wrong movements

(1) When stepping back, the feet end up in a straight line or "twisted".

(2) The hand movements and the foot movements are not completed simultaneously.

7. Grasping a Peacock's Tail on the Left Side

(1) Hold the hands and draw the feet

Turn the body slightly to the right. Move the right hand past the waist up backward to draw an arc and stop at the right chest; bend the right arm with the palm facing downward. Move the left hand down backward to draw an arc and stop in front of the abdomen with the palm facing up. The two palms face each other to form a ball-holding gesture. Draw the left foot beside the right foot and rest the toes on the floor. Look at the right hand. (Fig. 139)

(2) Turn the body and step up

Turn the torso slightly to the left, step forward to the left with the left foot, the heel pressing down on the floor. Look at the left hand. (Fig. 140)

(3) Bow step and straighten the arm

图 141 **Fig** 141

Keep turning the torso to the left. Shift the weight forward and place the left foot flat on the floor. Bend the left knee with the right leg straightened naturally to form a left bow step. Bend the left forearm in front of the chest with the palm facing inward. Drop the right hand and press beside the right hip, the palm facing downward and the fingers pointing forward. Look at the left hand. (Fig. 141)

(4) 转体摆臂:上体微向左转,左手向左上前伸出,掌心转向下;右臂外旋,右手经腹前向前,向上伸至左前臂内侧,掌心向上。眼看左手。(图 142)

图 142　　Fig 142

图 143　　Fig 143

(5) 转体后捋:上体右转,两手同时向下经腹前向右后方划弧后捋,右手举于身体侧后方,与头同高,掌心向前,左手举平屈于胸前,掌心向内;重心后移,身体后坐,右腿屈膝,左腿自然伸直,眼看右手。(图 143)

(6) 转体搭手:上体左转,正对前方;右臂屈肘,右前臂经面部搭于左腕内侧,掌心向前;左前臂仍屈于胸前,掌心向后,指尖向右;眼看右手。(图 144 ~ 146)

(4) Turn the torso and sway the arms

Turn the torso slightly to the left while extending the left hand forward with the palm turned town. Bring the right hand upward, the palm turning up, past abdomen until it is below the left forearm. Look at the left hand. (Fig. 142)

(5) Turn the torso and hands back

Turn the torso to the right while pulling both hands down in such a way as to draw an arc before the abdomen. Finish with the right hand extended sideways at head level, palm forward, and the left forearm bent across the chest, palm turned inward. At the same time shift the weight back, bend the right knee and stretch the left leg naturally. Look at the right hand.(Fig.143)

(6) Turn the torso and place the hand against the wrist

Turn the torso slightly to the left to face forward. Bend the right arm, bring the right forearm past the face and place it against the inside of the left wrist with the palm facing forward. Bend the left arm in front of the chest with the palm facing backward and the fingers pointing right. Look at the right hand.(Fig.144 – 146)

图 144 **Fig 144**

图 145 **Fig 145**

图 146 **Fig 146**

(7) 弓步前挤:重心前移,左腿屈弓,右腿自然蹬直成左弓步;右手推左前臂向体前挤出,与肩同高,两臂撑圆。眼看右腕。(图 147)

(8) 后坐引手:重心后移上体后坐,右腿屈膝,左腿自然伸直,左脚尖翘起;左手翻转向下,右手经左腕上方向前伸出,掌心向下,两手左右分开与肩同宽,两臂屈肘,弧线后引,经胸前收至腹前;眼向前平视。(图 148、149)

图 147　　Fig 147

图 148　　Fig 148

图 149　　Fig 149

(9) 弓步前按:重心前移,左脚踏实,左腿屈弓,右腿自然蹬直成左弓步;两手沿弧线向体前推按,两腕同肩高肩宽,掌心均向前,指尖向上。眼看前方。(图 150、151)

攻防含义

揽雀尾包括了太极拳中最基本的四种攻防手法:

掤手是屈臂迎架对方的来手,以观其变。在外形上与野马分鬃相似,其含义则完全不同。后者的进攻手法是分、靠,掤手则是接住对方来手,静观对方反应,以观其变。术语称为"懂劲"。

(7) "Bow step" and press forward

Shift the weight forward. Bend the left leg and straighten the right leg naturally to make a left bow step. The right hand pushes the left forearm and press forward at shoulder level and keep both arms rounded. Look at the right wrist. (Fig.147)

(8) Sit back and pull the hands

Shift the weight back, bend the right knee and straighten the left leg naturally with the left toes upward. Turn the left hand downward, extend the right hand past the left wrist forward with the palm facing downward. Separate the hands shoulder-width apart, bend both elbows to draw an arc back in front of the abdomen. Look straight ahead. (Fig.148 & 149)

(9) "Bow step" and push the hands forward

Shift the weight forward and place the left foot flat on the floor, bend the left leg, straighten the right leg naturally to form a left bow step while pushing the hands forward and obliquely up with the palms facing forward, until the wrists are shoulder high. Look forward. (Fig. 150 & 151)

图 150 Fig 150

图 151 Fig 151

The meaning of attack and defence

"Grasping a Peacock's Tail" includes the four basic ways to attack and defend in *taijiquan*:

捋是当对方攻来，一手附于其腕，另一手附于其肘关节，顺势向后牵引，同时转腰侧身，使其扑空。它与强拉不同之处在于不以力取胜，而是借力取巧，引进对手使其落空。

挤是当对方感到落空，急欲抽身后退之时，用前臂贴紧对方，用快速挤压之力攻击对方。

按的含义，在太极拳中常常在向前用力之前，先向下牵引对方使其向上反抗，重心升高，立脚不稳，再快速发力前推，取得更大效果。这种变化的用力称为按或前按。

练习要点

(1) 练习此势时，要注意上下肢的协调配合。掤、按时要与弓步一致；捋手和引手要与屈腿后坐一致。前弓腿和后坐时，重心移动要充分，上体要保持松正舒展。

(2) 此势是顺弓步的步型，练习时两脚间的横向距离以10厘米左右为宜。第一动的抱球收脚，脚尖着地应逐渐过渡到提收右脚内侧，脚尖不点地。

易犯错误

(1) 掤和按的动作，两臂不松展，出现紧张夹腋或松软无力现象。

(2) 前按时两手向两侧分开划弧或两掌自下划弧上挑。

(3) 手脚配合不协调，手快脚慢或脚快手慢。

HOLD—When the opponent attacks with hands, bend your arms to hit him/her back and wait to see what action she/he is going to take. In "Parting a Wild Horse's Mane on Both Sides" you hold the opponent's wrist and ram forward to attack.

PULL—When the opponent attacks, hold his/her wrist with one hand and press his/her elbow with the other hand, then pull the opponent back and stand aside at the same time to make him/her face to ground.

PRESS—When the opponent attacks and fails and decides to escape, press him/her with your arm to attack him/her.

PUSH—When you pull the opponent downward to make him/her lose his/her balance, push him/her with force.

Points to remember

(1) Coordinate separation of the hands relaxation with the waist and bending of the legs.

(2) When making bow steps, the parallel distance between the two feet is about 10cm. When drawing one foot beside the other, try to transfer from resting the toes on the floor to off the floor.

Wrong movements

(1) Press the arms against the sides instead of keeping both arms rounded.

(2) When pressing, the two hands part and each moves in an arc at the side, or the palms curve up.

(3) Hands and feet do not coordinate.

8. 右揽雀尾

(1) 转体分手：重心后移，右脚尖内扣，身体右转；右手经头前划弧右摆，掌心向外，两手平举于身体两侧，目光随右手转移。(图 152)

(2) 抱手收脚：左腿屈膝，重心左移，右脚收至左脚内侧，脚尖点地；左手屈肘至胸前，掌心向下，右手向下划弧至腹前，左右手下下相对抱球，眼看左手。(图 153)

图 152　Fig 152

图 153　Fig 153

图 154　Fig 154

(3) 转体上步：动作、方法同左揽雀尾，方向相反。(图 154)

(4) 弓步掤臂。(图 155)

(5) 转体展臂。(图 156)

(6) 转体后捋。(图 157)

(7) 转体搭臂。(图 158、159)

图 155　Fig 155

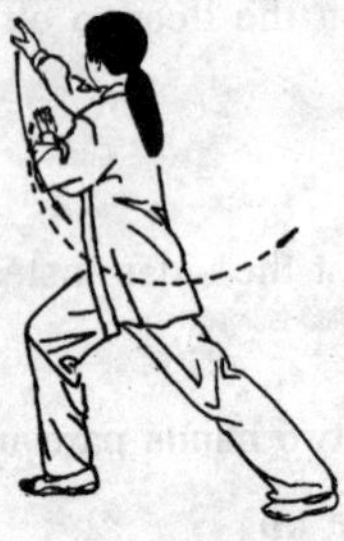

图 156　Fig 156

8. Grasping a Peacock's Tail on the Right Side

(1) Turn the body and move the hands apart

Sit back and turn the torso to the right, turning the toes of the right foot inward. Move the right hand past the head in an arc to the right with the palm facing outward. Move both hands up with the wrists at shoulder level. The eyes follow the right hand. (Fig. 152)

(2) Hold the hands and draw one foot beside the other

Bend the left knee, shift the weight to the left leg and move the right foot beside the left foot with the toes of the right foot resting on the floor. Bend the left elbow to the front of the chest with the palm facing downward while moving the right hand downward to the abdomen, the palms facing each other to form a ball-holding gesture with the left hand on top. Look at the left hand. (Fig. 153)

(3) Turn the body and move the step up: The movements are the same as those in Grasping a Peacock's Tail on the Left Side, but in opposite direction. (Fig. 154)

(4) Bow step and straighten the arms (Fig. 155)

(5) Turn the body and extend the arms (Fig. 156)

(6) Turn the body and pull back (Fig. 157)

(7) Turn the body and press the hand against the arm (Fig. 158 & 159)

图 157 **Fig** 157

图 158 **Fig** 158

图 159 **Fig** 159

(8) 弓步前挤。(图 160)

(9) 后坐引手。(图 161、162)

图 160　Fig 160

图 161　Fig 161

图 162　Fig 162

(10) 弓步前按。(图 163、164)

图 163　Fig 163

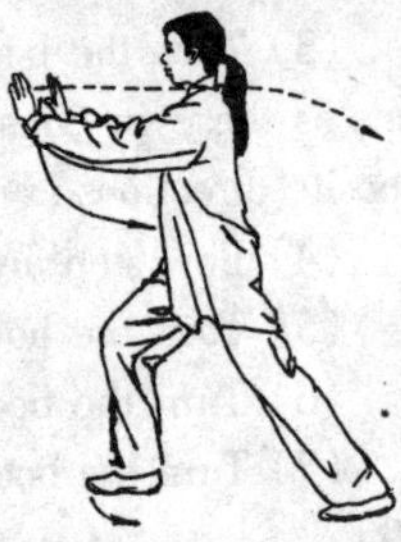
图 164　Fig 164

练习要点

(1) 身体后转,右手水平向后划弧,两手分开不超过 120°,左手不要随转体而向右摆动。

(2) 身体右转时,重心移向右腿,抱球收脚时重心移向左脚,身体左右平移不要上下起伏。左脚内扣的角度要大于 90°。

9. 单鞭

(1) 转体运臂:重心左移,上体左转,右脚尖内扣;两臂交叉划弧;左手经头前向左划弧至身体左侧,掌心向外,右手经腹前向左划弧至左肋前,掌心向内,眼随手转移。(图 165)

(8) Bow step and press forward(Fig.160)

(9) Sit back and draw the hand(Fig.161 & 162)

(10) Bow step and press forward(Fig.163 & 164)

Points to remember

(1) When the body turns to the back, move the right hand in a horizontal arc to the right and the angle made by the hands is not wider than 120 degrees. While the body turns, the left hand does not need to follow it to the right.

(2) When turning the body to the right, shift the weight to the right leg. Shift the weight back to the left leg while making a ball-holding gesture. Do not move the torso up and down while shifting the weight. Turn the left foot inward to make an angle wider than 90 degrees.

图 165 **Fig** 165

9. Single Whip

(1) Turn the body and move the arms

Shift the weight to the left, turn the torso to the left and the toes of the right foot inward. Cross both arms to draw an arc. Move the left hand in an arc past the forehead to the left, the palm facing outward, and the right hand past the abdomen in front of the left ribs, the palm facing inward. The eyes follow the hands.(Fig.165)

(2) 勾手收脚：上体右转，重心右移，右腿屈膝，左脚收至右脚内侧，脚尖点地；右手向上向右经头前划弧，掌心向内，在身体右侧前方变成勾手，腕与肩平；左手向下向右划弧经腹前至右肩前，掌心转向内，眼看右手。(图 166、167)

图 166 **Fig 166**

图 167 **Fig 167**

(3) 转体上步：上体稍左转，左脚向左前方上步，脚跟着地；左手经面前向左划弧，掌心向内；眼看左手。(图 168)

(4) 弓步推掌：身体左转，重心前移，左脚踏实，左膝屈膝，右腿自然蹬直，脚跟外展成稍向左前方的弓步。左手经面前翻掌向前推掌，腕与肩平，左肘与左膝、左脚尖上下成一条直线。眼看左手。(图 169)

(2) "Hooked hand" and draw the foot up

Turn the torso to the right. Shift the weight gradually onto the right leg. Bend the right knee and draw the left foot next to the right foot and rest the left toes on the floor. At the same time move the right hand in an arc upward and around to the right until the wrist is at shoulder level. Bend the right wrist to form a "hooked hand" while the left hand moves in an arc past the abdomen and pauses in front of the right shoulder, the palm facing inward. Look at the right hand. (Fig. 166 & 167)

(3) Turn the body and draw the step up

Turn the body slightly to the left, and step forward to the left with the left foot. Move the left hand past the forehead to the left in an arc, the palm facing inward. Look at the left hand. (Fig. 168)

(4) Bow step and push the hand

Turn the body slightly to the left, shift the weight forward and bend the left knee into a bow step, with the right leg straightened naturally. Rotate the left palm slowly and push it ahead with the wrist at shoulder level. The left elbow, left knee and toes of the left foot should be on a vertical line. Look at the left hand. (Fig. 169)

图 168　**Fig** 168

图 169　**Fig** 169

攻防含义

用法是我用右勾手叼住对方的手腕，再用左手出击。

练习要点

(1) 单鞭的弓步应稍斜向左前方，约15°~30°。两脚宽相距在30厘米左右。弓步时右脚跟外展，右腿蹬直，不可横裆开胯。

(2) 前臂、前腿方向一致，勾手的手腕与肩高，肘低于腕，勾尖向下，方向为斜后方，不可挺胸耸肩。

易犯错误

(1) 勾手时腕部放松故意旋转，形成“腕花”，五指不同时捏拢；腕关节僵直，勾尖向后。

(2) 弓步定势时，右脚跟蹬转不够，上体侧倾。

(3) 定势时易出现挺胸塌腰或身体前俯的错误。

10. 云手

(1) 转体松勾：重心右移，上体右转，左脚尖内扣；左手向下向右划弧，经腹前至右肩前，掌心向内；右勾手松开变掌，掌心向外；眼看右手。(图170、171)

图170　Fig 170

图171　Fig 171

The meaning of attack and defence

Use the right hand to hook the opponent's wrist and hit him/her with the left hand.

Points to remember

(1) Bend the left leg obliquely forward to the left to make an angle of 15 to 30 degrees. The distance between the two feet is about 30cm. Straighten the right leg with the heel outward.

(2) The front arm and front leg are in the same direction. Keep the wrist of the "hooked hand" at shoulder level and the elbow lower than the wrist with the hook downward and obliquely backward.

Wrong movements

(1) Twist the wrist while making a "hooked hand". Do not get all the fingers together simultaneously. The wrist is stiff and the hook of the "hooked hand" faces backward.

(2) When making a bow step, the torso turns forward and the right heel is not at the right position.

(3) When pausing, the waist is stiff or the torso turns forward.

10. Waving Hands like Clouds

(1) Turn the body and get the "hooked hand" loose

Shift the weight onto the right leg, turn the torso gradually to the right, and turn the toes of the left foot inward. Move the left hand in an arc past the abdomen to the front of the right shoulder with the palm turned inward. At the same time open the right hand and turn the palm outward. Look at the right hand. (Fig. 170 & 171)

(2) 左云手收步:上体左转,重心左移,左膝屈膝,右脚向左脚收拢,脚前掌先着地,随之全脚掌着地,两腿半蹲,两脚平行向前,相距 5~10 厘米成并步;左手经面前向左划弧运行,掌心由内慢慢转向外,停于身体左侧,腕与肩平,右手向下经腹前向左划弧停于左肩前,掌心向内;眼看左手。(图 172、173)

图 172　　Fig 172

图 173　　Fig 173

(3) 右云手开步:上体右转,重心移向右腿,左脚向左横开一步,脚前掌先着地,随之全脚踏实,脚尖向前;右手经头前向右划弧云转,掌心逐渐翻转向外,左手经腹前向下向右划弧云转,掌心逐渐转向内。右掌停于身体右侧,高与肩平,左手停于右肩前;眼看右手。(图 174、175)

(2) Wave the left hand like clouds and draw the foot back

Shift the weight gradually onto the left leg. Bring the right foot parallel to the left foot, about 5 to 10 cm apart. Arc the left hand past the face with the palm turning slowly outward and stop at the left side of the body with the wrist at shoulder level. Move the right hand in a curve past the abdomen and then upward to the left shoulder with the palm turned inward. Look at the left hand. (Fig. 172 & 173)

(3) Wave the right hand like clouds and move a step apart

Turn the torso rightward and shift the weight onto the right leg. Step the left foot sideward. Move the right hand to the right side, the palm turned outward, while the left hand makes an arc past the abdomen and downward to the right, the palm turned inward. Stop the right palm at the right side of the body as high as the shoulder and the left hand in front of the right shoulder. The eyes follow the right hand. (Fig. 174 & 175)

图 174　　Fig 174

图 175　　Fig 175

(4) 左云手并步：上体左转，重心左移，左脚向右脚并拢，脚前掌先着地，随之全脚踏实，两腿屈腿半蹲，两脚平行脚尖向前，两脚相距约 5 至 10 厘米；左手经头前向左划弧云转，掌心向外翻转，右手向下经腹前同时向左划弧云转，掌心逐渐翻转向内；左掌停于身体左侧，高与肩平，右掌停于左肩前，视线随左手转移。（图 176、177）

图 176　　Fig 176

图 177　　Fig 177

(5) 同第 3 动。（图 178、179）

图 178　　Fig 178

图 179　　Fig 179

(6) 同第 4 动。（图 180、181）

(4) Wave the left hand like clouds and bring the left foot parallel to the right foot

Turn the torso leftward and shift the weight onto the left leg, bring the left foot parallel to the right foot, about 5 – 10cm apart. Arc the left hand past the face with the palm turning slowly outward. Move the right hand in a curve past the abdomen and then upward to the left with the palm turned obliquely inward. Stop the left palm at the left side of the body as high as the shoulder and the right palm in front of the left shoulder. The eyes follow the left hand. (Fig. 176 & 177)

(5) Wave the right hand like clouds and move a step apart

Repeat movements in (3). (Fig. 178 & 179)

(6) Wave the left hand like clouds and bring the left foot parallel to the right foot

Repeat movements in (4). (Fig. 180 & 181)

图 180 **Fig** 180

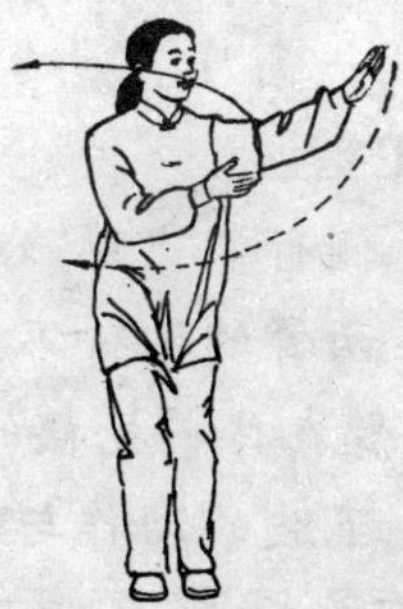

图 181 **Fig** 181

攻防含义

云手是防守动作,用前臂或手拨开对方的进攻。对方用左、右手连续进攻,我则用云手连续破解对方。也可以用右手拨开对方的右手后,左手插入对方腋下,向右横挒进攻。

练习要点

(1) 云手的手法是两手不同方向的向左或向右划立圆,同时两臂旋转翻掌。两手经面前和腹前不要太近或太远。

(2) 云手的步法是侧行步,侧行步要注意"点起点落"、"轻起轻落"的步法规律,两脚由脚跟提起,脚尖离地;落地时,脚尖先落然后全脚踏实,两腿轮换支撑体重。重心移动要充分,虚实要分明。移动时上体不可俯仰歪斜或摆晃;身体不起伏,重心要平稳,均匀运动,拳架保持同一高度。

易犯错误

(1) 侧行步出现"八字脚"或两脚靠拢的错误。

(2) 两臂的运行不是在腰的带动下运转,形成腰不转动,两臂在体前抡摆的错误。

(3) 下肢的动作与手臂的动作没有协调一致,时间上配合有前后,造成上下肢脱节。

(4) 扭摆腰胯。

The meaning of attack and defence

Waving hands like clouds is a means of defence. Defend yourself with your forearm or hand. When the opponent attacks constantly with both the right and left hands, wave your hands like clouds to defend yourself. You can also hit away the opponent's right hand with your right hand and thrust your left hand into the opponent's armpit to attack.

Points to remember

(1) Arm movements should be natural and circular and simultaneous with hand movements. When moving the two hands past the face or abdomen, keep a proper distance from it.

(2) When moving the steps sideward, remember to "rest the toes on/off the floor lightly". Raise the heel first, then the toes. When placing the foot on the floor, place the toes first and then the heel. Take turns to shift the weight from one leg to the other. When moving the steps, you should keep the torso erect, the body height even, the weight shift stable, and the movements smooth.

Wrong movements

(1) Move one foot sideward with the toes either inward or outward.

(2) Arm movements do not follow waist movements.

(3) Arm movements do not coordinate with leg movements.

(4) Turn the waist and hips while doing the movements.

11. 单鞭

(1) 转体勾手：上体右转，重心移向右腿，左脚跟提起；右手经头前向右划弧至右前方，掌心翻转变勾手，左手向下经腹前向右划弧，云转至右肩前，掌心转向内。眼看右手。(图 182)

(2) 转体上步：上体左转，左脚向左前方上步，脚跟落地；左手经面前向左划弧，掌心向内；眼看左手。(图 183)

(3) 弓步推掌：上体继续左转，重心前移，左脚踏实，左膝屈弓，右腿自然蹬直，脚跟外展，成斜向左前方的弓步；左手经面前翻转向前推出，腕与肩平，左肘对左膝。眼看左手。(图 184)

图 182　Fig 182

图 183　Fig 183

图 184　Fig 184

11. Single Whip

(1) Turn the body and form a hooked hand

Turn the body to the right and shift the weight onto the right leg with the left heel up. Move the right hand past the head to the right to draw an arc and turn the palm downward to make a hooked hand. Arc the left hand past the abdomen and then upward to the right shoulder, the palm turned inward. Look at the right hand. (Fig. 182)

(2) Turn the body and draw the foot up

Turn the body to the left and step leftward with the left foot, with the heel on the ground. Arc the left hand past the abdomen to the left, the palm turned inward. Look at the left hand. (Fig. 183)

(3) Bow step and push hand

Keep turning the body to the left, shifting the weight forward and placing the left foot flat on the floor. Bend the left knee, with the right leg straightened naturally and the right heel outward to make a left bow step. Rotate the left palm and push it ahead with the wrist at the same level of the shoulder. Keep the left elbow and the left knee on a verticle line. Look at the left hand. (Fig. 184)

12. 高探马

(1) 后脚跟步:后脚向前收半步,脚前掌着地,距前脚约一脚长;左臂略向前伸长,腕关节放松,掌心向下。(图 185)

(2) 后坐翻手:上体稍右转,重心后移,右脚踏实,右腿屈坐,左脚跟提起;右勾手松开,两手翻转向上,两臂前后平举,两臂微屈。眼看右手。(图 186)

图 185　　Fig 185

图 186　　Fig 186

(3) 虚步推掌:上体左转,右肩前送,右手经头侧向前推出,腕与肩高,掌心向前;左臂屈收,左手横至腹前,掌心向上,眼看右手;左脚稍向前移,脚前掌着地成左虚步。(图 187、188)

12. High Pat on Horse

(1) Move the back foot up

Move the back foot a half step forward and place the front sole on the floor with a distance of one foot behind the front foot. Extend the left arm slightly forward, relax the wrist with the palm facing downward. (Fig. 185)

(2) Sit back and turn the hand

Turn the torso slightly to the right, shift the weight backward and place the right foot flat on the floor. Bend the right leg and raise the left heel. Open the right hand and turn both palms upward with the elbows slightly bent. Look at the right hand. (Fig. 186)

(3) "Weak" step and push hand

Turn the torso slightly to the left and move the right shoulder forward. Draw the right hand past the right ear and push it forward with the palm facing forward. Lower the left arm and move the left hand to the front of the abdomen, the palm facing upward. Look at the right hand. Move the left foot slightly forward and place the front sole on the floor to make a left "weak" step. (Fig. 187 & 188)

图 187 **Fig** 187

图 188 **Fig** 188

攻防含义

当对方右拳或右掌击来，我用左前臂外旋压住其腕或前臂，并顺势向下向右引带，右手乘势直击其面，又称扑面掌。

练习要点

(1) 虚步推掌应在转腰顺肩的配合下完成，身体保持中正、舒展，动作协调一致。

(2) 后坐翻掌时，头随身体稍右转，眼睛向右前方扫视，不要过分转头看侧后方的右手，造成颈部过度旋转。

易犯错误

(1) 右臂前推时过分靠紧身体，夹肋紧腹。

(2) 虚步时，两腿过于伸直，重心过高。

(3) 身体后坐时，过分转头看后方的右手，造成歪头扭颈。

13. 右蹬脚

图 189　　Fig 189

(1) 收脚穿掌：上体稍右转，右手稍向后收，左手经右手背向右前方穿出，两手交叉，腕关节相交，左掌心斜向上，右掌心斜向下；左脚提起收至右小腿内侧；眼看左手。(图 189)

The meaning of attack and defence

When the opponent attacks with his/her right fist or right palm, move your left forearm outward to press his/her wrist or forearm and draw him/her downward to the right. Slap his/her face with your right hand.

Points to remember

(1) When making a "weak" step and pushing the hands forward, hold the torso erect and relaxed.

(2) When sitting back and turning the hands, the head follows the body slightly to the right. Look forward to the right instead of at the right hand.

Wrong movements

(1) When pushing the right hand forward, press the right arm tightly against the body.

(2) Straighten the two legs when making a "weak" step.

(3) When sitting back, turn back the bead too much to look at the right hand, making the head and neck slant.

13. Kicking with the Right Heel

(1) Draw the foot and cross the hands

Turn the torso slightly to the right, draw the right hand slightly backward and place the left hand, the palm obliquely upward, onto the back of the right wrist to cross the hands and wrists, the right plam bliquely downward. Raise the left foot and move it beside the right leg. Look at the left hand. (Fig. 189)

(2) 上步翻手：上体稍左转，左脚向左前方迈出，脚跟着地；两手翻转分开，掌心向前，虎口相对，两臂半屈成弧形相对；眼看前方。（图 190）

图 190　　Fig 190

图 191　　Fig 191

(3) 弓步分手：重心前移，左脚踏实成左弓步，右腿自然蹬直；两手向两侧划弧，掌心向外。眼看前方。（图 191）

(4) 收脚合抱：右脚收至左脚内侧，脚尖点地；两手向下划弧至腹前相交合抱，右手在下，掌心向左；眼看前方。（图 192、193）

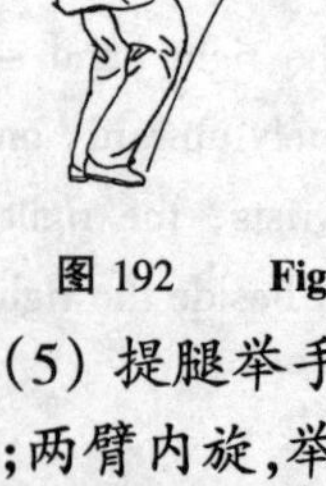

图 192　　Fig 192

图 193　　Fig 193

(5) 提腿举手：左腿支撑，右腿屈膝上提，右脚尖自然下垂；两臂内旋，举于胸前；眼看右前方。（图 194）

(2) Step up and turn the hands

Turn the torso slightly to the left. Move the left foot forward to the left and place the heel on the floor. Separate the hands with the palms facing forward. Slightly bend the two elbows to make an arc. Look forward. (Fig. 190)

(3) Bow step and separate the hands

Shift the weight forward and place the left foot flat on the floor to make a left bow step with the right leg straightened naturally. Move the hands in a downward arc with the palms turned outward. Look forward. (Fig. 191)

(4) Draw the foot and "hold" with both hands

Draw the right foot beside the left foot with the toes resting on the floor. Move both hands downward in a circle until they cross in front of the abdomen with the right hand below and the palm facing left. Look forward. (Fig. 192 & 193)

(5) Raise the leg and turn the hands

Raise the right leg and bend the right knee with the toes naturally facing downward. Rotate both arms inward up to the front of the chest. Look forward. (Fig. 194)

图 194　　**Fig** 194

图 195　　Fig 195

(6) 蹬脚分手：右脚脚尖上勾，脚跟用力慢慢向前蹬出，右腿膝关节伸直，与右臂上下相对，方向为右前方约 30°，眼看右手；两手分别向右前和左后方划弧分手，两臂展开两侧，肘关节微屈，腕与肩平，掌心皆向外。(图 195)

攻防含义

用两手分拨开对方的进攻，随后用脚蹬踹对方。

练习要点

(1) 此势的动作较难，练习要做到“稳”和“协调”。

稳：首先收脚时脚尖可点地，调整重心到位，逐步做到收脚不点地的平稳状态；提膝、蹬脚的动作要匀速缓慢，不可加速，防止失去平衡，保证重心稳定。

协调：要做到六个一致。收脚和穿掌一致；上步和翻手一致；弓步与分手一致；收脚与抱手一致；提膝与举抱一致；蹬脚与分手撑臂一致。练习时，六个一致能很好的完成，整个右蹬脚就会协调的完成。

(2) 本势的手臂的动作较复杂，练习时注意“穿掌——分手——合抱——分手撑臂”的过程中两手两次交叉和分开，注意划弧的路线和前臂旋转等细节。

易犯错误

(1) 单脚站不稳，上体后仰或前倾，两臂一高一低。

(6) Kick the foot and separate the hands

Raise the toes of the right foot up and kick the heel gently forward to the right to make an angle of about 30 degrees, with the right knee straightened and below the right arm. Look at the right hand. Separate the hands, extending them sideways in an arc at shoulder level, the palms turned outward. (Fig. 195)

The meaning of attack and defence

Use your hands to fend against the opponent's attack and kick him/her with the heel.

Points to remember

(1) Balance and coordination are essential in this form.

To keep balance: You can rest your toes on the floor to keep your balance when drawing one foot next to the other. Then try to learn to draw one foot next to the other without resting your toes on the floor to keep balance. Bend the knee and kick with the heel gently in order to keep balance.

To coordinate the movements: Draw one foot next to the other and cross the hands simultaneously; step forward and turn the hands simultaneously; make a bow step and separate the hands simultaneously; draw one foot next to the other and move the hands outward in a circle simultaneously; bend the knee and move the hands outward in a circle simultaneously; kick forward with the heel and extend the arms simultaneously.

(2) Cross and separate the hands twice and pay attention to moving the arms in an arc or in a circle in "crossing hands — separating the hands — arcing the arms — extending the arms".

(2) 独立的左腿过于弯曲，蹬出的右腿勾脚尖不够，力点达不到脚跟。

(3) 右臂与右腿上下不相对应。

(4) 提肩缩脖，胸部憋气；低头弯腰。

上述错误的主要原因是全身紧张、用力勉强、身体素质达不到要求所致。练习时要根据自己的实际情况加强练习，循序渐进，逐步提高。

14. 双峰贯耳

(1) 屈膝并手：右小腿屈膝回收，脚尖自然下垂；左手经体侧向体前划弧，与右手并行落于右腿的上方，掌心皆翻转向上，指尖向前；眼看前方。(图 196)

(2) 上步落手：左腿屈膝，右脚向右前方上步，脚跟着地，脚尖斜向右前约 30°；两手收至两侧腰间，掌心向上。(图 197)

(3) 弓步掼拳：重心前移，右脚踏实，右腿屈弓，左腿自然蹬直成右弓步；两手握拳从两侧向上向前划弧至头前，两臂半屈成弧相对，两拳相对成钳形，相距同头宽，两前臂内旋，拳眼斜向下；眼看前方。(图 198)

图 196　Fig 196

图 197　Fig 197

图 198　Fig 198

Wrong movements

(1) Lose balance while standing on a single leg; fail to keep the torso erect and the two arms at the same level.

(2) Stand on an over-bent leg and kick without the toes upturned enough.

(3) The right arm does not parallel the right leg.

(4) Shrug the shoulders and bow with the head dropped.

To avoid the above wrong movements, keep the body relaxed and practise.

14. Striking the Opponent's Ears with Both Fists

(1) Bend the knee and put one hand next to the other

Pull the right foot back and suspend it, bending the knee with the thigh level horizontally. Move the left hand up and forward, then down next to the right hand, turning both palms up, with the fingertips pointing forward. Look forward. (Fig. 196)

(2) Step up and move both hands in an arc downward

Bend the left knee and move the right foot forward and rightward with the heel on the floor and the toes pointing obliquely forward to the right to make an angle of 30 degrees. Move both hands to the sides of the waist with the palms facing upward. (Fig. 197)

(3) Bow step and strike with the fists

Shift the weight forward and drop the right foot to the floor at a point slightly to the right front to form a bow step. At the same time drop both hands and gradually clench the fists. Then arc the hands upward and forward from the sides to the front, coming together at ear level in a pincerlike movement with head width, the knuckles facing obliquely upward. Look forward. (Fig. 198)

攻防含义

两拳自腰间同时向前上方划弧摆打,横击对方太阳穴。

练习要点

(1) 本势弓步的方向与右蹬脚的方向一致。在上步出脚前,左支撑腿先屈蹲,重心下降,然后再将右腿迈出,直到脚跟着地时重心仍在左腿。

(2) 两拳向前上方掼出,力量在拳面,两拳眼斜向下,立身中正,沉肩坠肘。

易犯错误

(1) 两手握拳过紧或过松

(2) 两肘抬起,拳眼向下或两臂平直,拳眼相对。

(3) 定式时,低头拱背,俯身突臀。

15. 转身左蹬脚

(1) 转体分手:重心左移,上体左转,右脚尖内扣;两拳松开,左手经头前随转体向左划弧,两臂微屈,侧举身体两侧,掌心向外,眼看左手。(图 199、200)

(2) 收脚合抱:重心右移,右腿屈膝后坐,左脚收至右脚内侧,脚尖点地;两臂向下划弧,于腹前交叉合抱,左手在后,手心向右;眼看前方。(图 201)

图 199　**Fig 199**

图 200　**Fig 200**

图 201　**Fig 201**

The meaning of attack and defence

Arc the fists from the sides of the waist up to the front to hit the opponent's temples.

Points to remember

(1) The bow step points to the same direction with the right foot. Bend the left knee and move forward with the right foot with the weight still on the left leg.

(2) Arc the fists upward and forward, knuckles facing left. Hold the head and neck erect; lower the shoulders and allow the elbows to fall naturally with the arms slightly bent.

Wrong movements

(1) Clench the fists either too tight or too loose.

(2) Straighten the arms to parallel the fists.

(3) Bow with the head dropped.

15. Turning and Kicking with the Left Heel

(1) Turn the body and separate the hands

Shift the weight leftward. Turn the torso to the left with the toes of the right foot pointing inward. Simultaneously open the fists and separate the hands in a circular movement, extending the hands sideways slightly above shoulder level, the palms facing outward. Look at the left hand. (Fig. 199 & 200)

(2) Shift the weight onto the right leg

Bend the right knee and shift the weight onto the right leg. Bring the left foot next to the right foot and rest the toes on the floor. At the same time circle both hands downward and cross the hands in front of the abdomen with the left hands back, the palm facing rightward. Look forward. (Fig. 201)

(3) 提膝提臂：左腿提膝高抬，脚尖自然下垂；两臂内旋，两掌心向内，举至胸前；眼看前方。（图 202、203）

图 202　　Fig 202

图 203　　Fig 203

(4) 分手蹬脚：两手向左前和右后翻转划弧分开，掌心皆向外平举于身体两侧，肘关节微屈；左脚尖勾屈，脚跟着力向左前方（约 30°）慢慢蹬出，与右蹬脚方向对称，左脚蹬直与左臂上下相对；眼看左手。（图 204、205）

攻防含义

左蹬脚用分手拨开对方的进攻，随即用脚蹬踹对方。

练习要点

(1) 两个蹬脚方向要对称，与中轴线前后保持约 30°的斜向。

(2) 转体分手时，上体保持正直，右脚尽量内扣，重心移动要充分。

易犯错误

转体时，重心移动不充分，右脚内扣角度不够，左右移重心不够，虚实不明。

(3) Lift the knee and raise the arms

Lift the left knee with the thigh up horizontally and drop the toes naturally. Move both hands in an arc inward and up to the level of the chest, the palms facing inward. Look forward. (Fig. 202 & 203)

(4) Separate the hands and kick with the heel

Separate the hands and extend them sideways at shoulder level, the palms facing outward and the elbows bent. Meanwhile, raise the left leg with the knee bent, then kick the foot slowly forward toward the left in an angle of 30 degrees. Straightened the left leg to parallel the left arm. Look at the left hand. (Fig. 204 & 205)

图 204 **Fig** 204

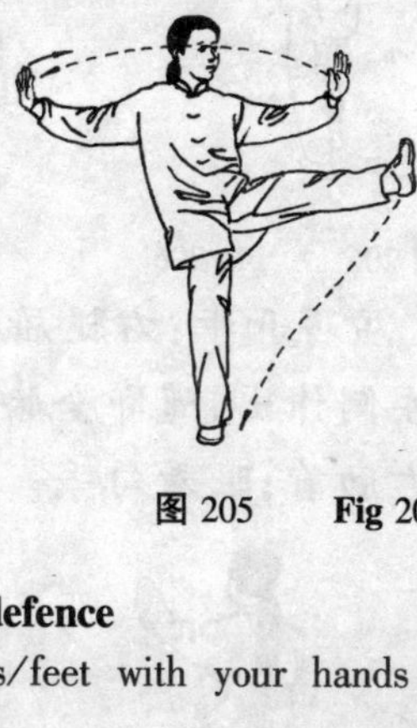

图 205 **Fig** 205

The meaning of attack and defence

Separate the opponent's hands/feet with your hands and kick him/her with your heel.

Points to remember

(1) The directions of kicking of the heels should be symmetrical in an angle of 30 degrees with the vertical line.

(2) Keep the torso erect while turning the body and separating the hands. Move the right sole inward and shift the weight right in position.

Wrong movements

Shift the weight not exactly right in position and move the right sole not inward enough.

16. 左下势独立

(1) 收脚勾手：左腿屈收，左脚尖下垂收于右小腿侧；上体微右转，右臂稍内合，右手捏拢变勾手，左手经头前划弧摆至右肩前，掌心向右，指尖向上；眼看右手。(图 206、207)

图 206　　Fig 206

图 207　　Fig 207

(2) 屈蹲开步：右腿屈膝半蹲，左脚脚前掌落地，沿地面向左侧伸出，随即全脚落实，左腿伸直成右弓步；左手落于右肋前；眼看勾手。(图 208、209)

图 208　　Fig 208

图 209　　Fig 209

(3) 仆步穿掌：右腿屈膝全蹲，上体左转成仆步；左手经腹前沿左腿内侧前穿出，掌心向外，指尖向脚的方向穿至左踝；眼看左手。(图 210)

16. Pushing Down and Standing on the Left Leg

(1) Place one foot next to the other and make a "hooked hand"

Pull the left foot back next to the right foot and point the toes naturally downward. Turn the torso slightly to the right. Move the right arm slightly inward to make a "hooked hand" with the right hand while arcing the left hand up to the right until it stops in front of the right shoulder, the palm facing to the right and the fingertips pointing upward. Look at the right hand. (Fig. 206 & 207)

(2) Crouch and step sideways

Crouch slowly on the right leg, stretching the left leg sideways, placing the left foot flat on the floor and straightening the left leg to make a right bow step. Extend the left hand sideways and stop it in front of the right ribs. Look at the hooked hand. (Fig. 208 & 209)

(3) Bend the right leg in a full crouch and shuttle the left palm

图 210 **Fig** 210

Bend the right leg in a full crouch, turn the right toes slightly outward and straighten the left leg with the left toes turned slightly inward, both soles flat on the floor. Keep the toes of the left foot in line with the heel of the right foot. Turn the torso slightly to the left. At the same time shuttle the left palm along the inner side of the left leg until it reaches the ankle, the fingers pointing to the foot and the palm facing outward. Look at the left hand. (Fig. 210)

(4) 弓步起身：重心移向左腿，左脚尖外撇，左腿屈膝前弓，右脚尖内扣，右腿自然蹬直，重心恢复至弓步的高度；左手继续前穿并向上挑起至胸高，右手内旋，背于身后，勾尖朝上；眼看左手。(图 211)

图 211 Fig 211

图 212 Fig 212

(5) 独立挑掌：上体微右转，重心前移，右腿屈膝前提至腹前，脚尖自然下垂，左腿微屈独立支撑，成左独立步；左手下落按于左胯旁，右勾手下落变掌，掌心向内，经体侧向体前挑起掌心向左，指尖向上，高与眼平，右臂半屈成弧，肘关节与右膝相对；眼看右手。(图 212)

攻防含义

对方左手打来，我用右勾手刁住其腕，随之蹲身下势，左腿左掌插入对方裆下，将对方掀起；对方用右手击来，我用右掌向上排开对方，随即右腿屈提，用膝关节向前顶撞对方。

(4) Bow step and rise up

Shift the weight onto the left leg. Using the heel as pivot, turn the toes of the left foot slightly outward and bend the left knee. Turn the toes of the right foot inward while the right leg straightens. Shift the weight forward to make a left bow step. At the same time keep moving the left hand up till the level of the chest. Turn the right hand inward with the fingertips of the hooked hand pointing upward. Look at the left hand. (Fig.211)

(5) Stand on one leg and poke the palm

Turn the torso slightly to the right and shift the weight forward. Raise the right foot gradually and bend the right knee so that the thigh is raised horizontally with the toes naturally pointing downward. Bend the left leg slightly and stand on it. Lower the left hand to press at the side of the left hip, open the right hand, the palm facing inward, and poke the right palm past the outer side of the right leg, then upward to the front, the palm facing leftward and the fingertips pointing upward. Bend the right arm slightly and the elbow parallels the right knee. look at the right hand. (Fig.212)

The meaning of attack and defence

When the opponent attacks with his/her left hand, hook his/her wrist with your right hand. At the same time crouch and thrust your left hand and left foot between his/her legs to throw him/her down. When the opponent hits with his/her right hand, ward it off with your right palm, raise your right foot and bend your right knee to press against the opponent with your right knee.

练习要点

(1) 仆步时步型要正确。仆步的两脚前后应保持一脚长的距离,以仆步出腿的脚尖和下蹲腿的脚跟置于中轴线上为宜,重心由仆步转向前弓腿时,两脚要依次尽量外撇和内扣,保持重心平稳,完成独立提膝动作。

(2) 向左穿掌时,左臂先屈后伸,上体微向前倾,完成穿掌动作。

(3) 定势时,右臂要舒展撑圆,左手向下沉按,左臂微屈;独立腿微屈站稳,前腿大腿高于水平,上体保持舒展正直。

易犯错误

(1) 屈蹲开步时眼看左侧,转头过早,上体倾斜。

(2) 仆步时左脚掌外侧"掀脚",右脚跟离地"拢跟"。

(3) 由仆步转弓腿时,右脚不是脚尖内扣,而是后蹬外展,造成两脚距离过大,屈膝提腿困难;右脚外撇不够,造成独立支撑不稳,上体紧张歪扭。

17. 右下势独立

图 213　　**Fig** 213

(1) 落地勾手:右脚落于左脚内侧前方,脚前掌着地,左脚以脚跟为轴向左转体;左手上提成勾手举于身体左侧,高与肩平,右手经头前划弧摆至左肩前,掌心向右,指尖向上;眼看左手。(图 213)

Points of remember

(1) When one leg is bent in a full crouch, turn the toes slightly outward, straighten the other leg with the toes turned slightly inward and place both soles flat on the floor with a distance of one foot.

(2) When shuttling the left palm leftward, bend the left arm first and then extend it. Lean the torso slightly forward.

(3) When extending the right arm, bend the right elbow slightly. When moving the left hand downward, bend the left elbow slightly. When standing on one leg, bend the standing leg slightly, raise the thigh higher than horizontal level and keep the torso upright.

Wrong movements

(1) When crouching, move the head leftward too early and make the body lean to one side

(2) When turning the left foot outward, do not place the outer side of the left sole on the floor, meanwhile raise the right heel off the floor.

(3) When making a bow step from crouching, instead of turning the toes of the right foot inward, turn the heel outward, making the distance between the two soles too wide so that it is difficult to raise the leg and bend the knee. Keep the toes of the left foot straight forward, making it hard to stand on the left leg.

17. Pushing Down and Standing on the Right Leg

(1) Place the foot on the floor and make a "hooked hand"

Place the right foot in front of the left and rest the front sole on the floor. Turn the body to the left, using the left heel as a pivot and turning the left foot outward slightly. At the same time raise the left hand sideways up to shoulder level, forming a hooked hand, while the right hand, following the torso, moves in an arc to the front of the left shoulder, the palm facing right and the fingers pointing up. Look at the left hand. (Fig.213)

图 214　　Fig 214

(2) 屈蹲开步：左腿屈膝半蹲，右脚提收至左小腿内侧，然后以脚前掌着地，沿地面向右伸出，随即右腿伸直，右脚全脚掌蹲实；右手落至右肋前。眼看左手。(图 214)

(3) 仆步穿掌：左腿屈膝全蹲，上体右转成右仆步；右手经腹前沿右腿内侧向右穿出，掌心向外，指尖向脚的方向；眼看右手。(图 215、216)

图 215　　Fig 215

图 216　　Fig 216

(4) 弓步起身：重心移向右腿，右脚尖外撇，右腿屈膝前弓，左脚尖内扣，左腿自然蹬直，重心恢复至弓步高度；右手继续前穿并向上挑起至胸高，左手内旋，背向体后，勾尖向上；眼看右手。(图 217)

图 217　　Fig 217

(5) 独立挑掌：上体右转，重心前移，左腿屈膝前提，脚尖下垂，右腿微屈独立支撑成右独立步；右手下落按于右胯旁，左勾手下落变掌，经体侧向体前挑起，掌心向右，指尖向上，高与眼平，左臂半屈成弧，肘关节与左膝相对；眼看左手。(图 218)

(2) Crouch and step sideways

Bend the left knee, move the right foot to the inner side of the left leg and place the front sole of the right foot on the floor. Move the right foot rightward, straighten it and place the right foot flat on the floor. Pull the right hand in front of the left rib. Look at the left hand. (Fig.214)

(3) Bend the left leg in a full crouch and shuttle the right palm

Bend the left leg in a full crouch and turn the torso leftward in a right crouching stance. Shuttle the right palm sideways past the abdomen along the inner side of the right leg and up, the palm facing outward with the fingertips forward. Look at the right hand. (Fig 215 & 216)

(4) Bow step and rise up

Shift the weight onto the right leg, turn the toes of the right foot slightly outward and bend the right knee. Turn the toes of the left foot inward while the left leg straightens to make a right bow step. At the same time extend the right hand forward and up to the level of the chest. Turn the left hand inward and back with the fingertips of the hooked hand upward. Look at the right hand. (Fig.217)

图 218 **Fig** 218

(5) Stand on one leg and poke the palm

Turn the torso to the right and shift the weight forward. Raise the left foot gradually and bend the left knee so that the thigh is level horizontally, the toes pointing downward naturally. Bend the standing right leg slightly. Lower the right hand to press at the side of the right hip. At the same time open the left hand and poke the palm past the outer side of the left leg, then upward to the front, with the fingertips up and the palm facing rightward at the level of the eyes. Arc the left arm and the elbow parallels the left knee. Look at the left hand. (Fig.218)

练习要点

(1) 第一动右脚应落在左脚右侧前方约 20 厘米处，两脚保持一定的距离，便于转动。

(2) 向左转体后，重心应落在左腿。

易犯错误

(1) 第一动落脚转体重心没落在左腿上。

(2) 左手右手在转体时不同时的提起或划弧，造成上下肢脱节。

18. 左右穿梭

1) 右穿梭

(1) 落脚抱手：左脚向左前方落脚，脚跟着地，上体左转；左手翻转向下，右手翻转向上，两手在左肋前上下相抱；眼看左手。（图 219、220）

图 219　Fig 219

图 220　Fig 220

Points to remember

(1) Place the right foot 20 cm forward to the right of the left foot and keep a certain distance between the two feet.

(2) After turning the body to the left, shift the weight onto the left leg.

Wrong movements

(1) After turning the body to the left, the weight is not shifted onto the left leg.

(2) Both hands do not raise up and arc simultaneously while turning the body.

18. Working Shuttles on Both Sides

1) Working Shuttles on the Right Side

(1) Place the foot on the floor and make a ball-holding gesture

Place the left heel forward to the left on the floor and turn the torso to the left. At the same time make a ball-holding gesture in front of the left rib with the left hand on top. Look at the left hand. (Fig. 219 & 220)

(2) Step forward and roll a "ball"

Turn the torso to the right. Then move the right foot beside the left foot obliquely forward with the heel on the floor. Raise the right hand forward in an arc and at the same time lower the left hand backward to make a ball-holding gesture with the left hand at the side of the waist, the palm facing forward and the fingertips pointing upward, and the

(2) 上步滚球:上体右转,右脚提收经左脚内侧斜前方上步,脚跟着地;右手由下向前上方划弧,左手由后下方划弧,两手抱球滚动,左手在腰间,掌心向前,指尖向上;右手在胸前,掌心向后,指尖向前;眼看右手。(图 221)

(3) 弓步架推:上体继续右转,重心前移,右脚踏实,右腿屈膝前弓成右弓步;右手翻转上举架于右额角前上方;左手推至体前,高与鼻平。眼看左手。(图 222)

图 221　　Fig 221

图 222　　Fig 222

2) 左穿梭

图 223　　Fig 223

(1) 转体后坐:重心后移,右脚尖抬起;右手下落于头前,左手稍向左划弧,落至腹前准备“抱球”,眼看右手。(图 223)

(2) 抱球收脚:两手在右肋前上下相抱,左脚收至右脚内侧,眼看右手。(图 224、225)

right hand in front of the chest, the palm facing backward and the fingertips pointing forward. Look at the right hand.(Fig. 221)

(3) Bow step and push forward

Keep turning the torso to the left. Shift the weight forward, step forward on the right foot to make a right bow step. At the same time move the right hand upward, pausing just above the right temple with the palm turned obliquely upward. Push the left hand forward at nose level, the palm facing forward. Look at the left hand.(Fig.222)

2) Working Shuttles on the Left Side

(1) Turn the torso and sit back

Shift the weight backward slightly, the toes of the right foot turned up. Meanwhile lower the right hand in front of the head and simultaneously move the left hand in an arc forward to the front of the abdomen, ready to make a ball-holding gesture. Look at the right hand.(Fig.223)

(2) Draw the foot up and make a ball-holding gesture

Make a ball-holding gesture in front of the right rib with the right hand on top. Place the left foot next to the right foot with the toes on the floor. Look at the right hand.(Fig.224 & 225)

图 224　　Fig 224

图 225　　Fig 225

(3) 上步滚动：上体左转，左脚向左斜前方上步，脚跟着地；左手由下向前上方划弧，右手由上向后下方划弧；左手在胸前，掌心向后，指尖向右，右手在腰间，掌心向前，指尖向上，两掌相对；眼看左手。(图 226)

(4) 弓步架推：上体继续左转，重心前移，左脚踏实，左腿屈膝前弓成左弓步；左手翻转上举，架于左额角前上方；右手推至体前，高与鼻平；眼看右手。(图 227)

图 226　　Fig 226

图 227　　Fig 227

攻防含义

对方右手打来，我伸右手向上挑架，同时左手前推攻击对方。左右用意相同。

练习要点

(1) 本式的手法变化是由“抱球”过渡为一手上撑，一手前推。两手的动作路线，恰似把抱在胸前的“球”向左(右)上方翻转滚动，由此开始上架前推。

(2) 由“右穿梭”接做“左穿梭”时，先后坐再跟步的转换方法与“左右搂膝拗步”差不多，但要注意右脚尖不要外撇。

(3) Step forward and roll a "ball"

Turn the torso to the left. Move the left foot forward toward the left and place the heel on the floor. Raise the left hand in an arc forward to the front of the chest, the palm facing backward while lower the right hand in an arc backward to the right side of the waist, the palm facing forward with the fingertips pointing upward. The two palms face each other. Look at the left hand. (Fig. 226)

(4) Bow step and push forward

Keep turning the torso to the left. Shift the weight forward on the left foot to make a left bow step. At the same time move the left hand upward, pausing just above the left temple with the palm turned obliquely upward. Push the right hand forward at nose level. Look at the right hand. (Fig. 227)

The meaning of attack and defence

When the opponent attacks with his/her right hand, raise your right hand to ward it off and at the same time attack him/her with your left hand.

Points to remember

(1) Transfer from a ball-holding gesture to one hand pushing upward and the other forward as if you are turning the "ball" with your hands.

(2) When ending "Working Shuttles on the Right Side" and starting "Working Shuttles on the Left Side", sit back first before moving the step, similar to the foot movement in "Brushing the knees and Twisting the Steps on Both Sides", but be careful not to have the right toes pointing outward too much.

(3) 左右穿梭是拗弓步推掌，弓步方向和推掌方向是一致的，与中轴线约成30°斜角。两脚的横向宽度保持在30厘米左右，两脚过窄影响重心稳定。上体要端正。

易犯错误

(1) 架掌时耸肩抬肘，上体歪扭。

(2) 定势时，推掌方向和弓步方向不一致。

(3) 左穿梭时，右脚尖外撇改变方向造成左腿上步困难。

19. 海底针

(1) 跟步提手：右脚向前收拢半步，脚前掌落地，距左脚约一脚长；随后重心后移，右腿屈膝后坐，上体右转，左脚跟提起；右手下落经体前至体右侧提抽至身旁，掌心向左，指尖向前；左手随向右转体划弧下落到右腹前，掌心向下，指尖向右，眼看前方。（图228～231）

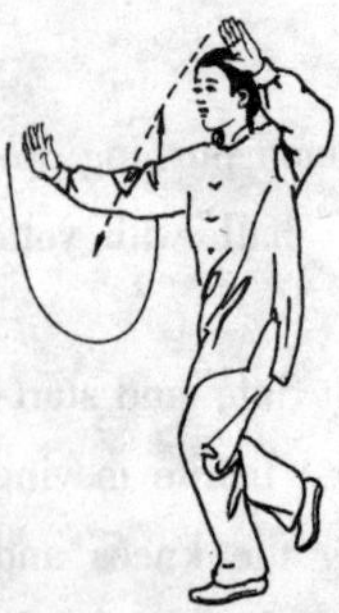

图 228　Fig 228

图 229　Fig 229

图 230　Fig 230

(3) When forming a ball-holding gesture, keep both the knee of the bow step and the palm facing the same direction and make an angle of 30 degrees with the vertical line. The parallel distance between the heels in the bow step is 30 cm.

Wrong movements

(1) Lift the shoulders when raising the hands.

(2) When pushing the hand forward, the knee of the bow step and the palm do not face the same direction.

(3) When working shuttles on the left side, move the toes of the right foot outward.

19. Needle at Sea Bottom

(1) Step forward and raise the hand

图 231 **Fig 231**

Move the right foot a half step forward and place the front sole on the floor with a distance of one foot from the front foot. Shift the weight back onto the right leg, bend the right leg and sit back. Turn the torso to the right and raise the left heel. Lower the right hand in front of the body, then raise it up beside the right ear, the palm facing leftward and the fingers pointing forward. Simultaneously move the left hand in an arc rightward and then down to the abdomen, the palm facing downward and the fingertips pointing rightward. Look forward. (Fig. 228 & 231)

图 232　　Fig 232

(2) 虚手插掌:上体左转,向前俯身;右手从耳侧向前下方斜插,掌心向左,指尖斜向下,左手经左膝前划弧搂过,按至大腿外侧;左脚稍前移,脚前掌着地成左虚步;眼看右手。(图 232)

攻防含义

当对方打来,我用左手搂开对方的手,右手直插对方裆部,用指尖戳击对方。

练习要点

(1) 虚步插掌时,上体要舒展伸拔,上体前倾角度不超过 30°。

(2) 两手动作的路线:随转体右手在体前至右侧划一个立圆;随转体左手在体前划半个圆。右手向上抽提应提到右耳旁,不要仅提到胸前,此时应保持松肩垂肘,不要因为右手上提而扬肘耸肩,身体歪斜。

(3) 定势时,形成虚步、右手下插和左手下按三者要同时完成。

易犯错误

(1) 右手下插时,易做成"前劈"或"下砍"动作。

(2) 定式时出现低头,弯腰。两腿虚实不清。

(3) 腰与肢体脱节,动作散乱,没有用腰部的转动来带动和协调全身的动作。

(2) Weak step and thrust the hands

Turn the torso to the left and lean forward. Thrust the right hand obliquely downward, the palm facing leftward and the fingertips obliquely downward. Move the left hand past the left knee in an arc and press at the outer side of the left hip. Move the left foot slightly forward with the front sole coming down on the floor to form a left "weak step". Look at the right hand. (Fig.232)

The meaning of attack and defence

When the opponent attacks, push his/her hand aside with your left hand and at the same time thrust your right hand and hit him/her at the crotch and poke him/her with your fingertips.

Points to remember

(1) Keep the torso erect when thrusting the hand downward and make an angle no wider than 30 degrees when leaning forward.

(2) First turn the body slightly to the right and move the right hand to draw a full arc on the right side simultaneously, then turn the body to the left and the left hand draws a semi-arc in front of the body. Raise the right hand to the right ear. Keep the torso relaxed and the shoulders dropped. Do not shrug the shoulders while raising the right hand.

(3) Make a "weak step", thrust the right hand downward and press the left hand simultaneously.

Wrong movements

(1) Chop the right hand obliquely forward instead of thrusting the right hand obliquely downward.

(2) Low the head down, bow or straighten the front leg while pausing.

(3) Do not pivot the waist to coordinate the movements.

20. 闪通臂

(1) 提手收脚:上体恢复正直,右腿屈膝支撑,左脚收回,以脚尖点地落在右脚内侧;右手上提至身前,指尖向前,掌心向左,左手屈臂上举,指尖贴于右腕内侧;眼看前方。(图 233)

(2) 弓步推撑:左脚前迈一步成左弓步;左手推至体前,与鼻尖对齐,掌心向前,右手撑于头侧上方,掌心斜向上,两手前后分展;眼看左手。(图 234、235)

图 233 Fig 233

图 234 Fig 234

图 235 Fig 235

练习要点

(1) 上下肢配合应协调一致,同时到位。

(2) 此势是顺弓步推掌,步子不可过宽;前手、前腿要上下相对;上体也不可过分扭转侧身。

21. 转身扳拦捶

(1) 转体扣脚:重心右移,右腿屈坐,左脚尖内扣;身体右转,两手向右侧摆动,右手摆至身体右侧,左手摆至左侧头旁,两手心向斜下方;眼看右手。(图 236)

20. Flashing the Arm

(1) Raise the hands and draw the leg up

Turn the torso erect. Bend the right leg to support the weight. Draw the left foot and place the toes on the floor next to the right foot. Raise the right hand to the front of the body, the fingertips pointing forward and the palm facing leftward. Bend the right arm and raise it up with the fingertips pressing against the inside of the right wrist. Look forward. (Fig. 233)

(2) Bow step and push the hand forward

Step forward with the left foot to form a left bow step. Raise the left hand and push it forward at nose level with the palm facing forward. Raise the right arm until the hand stops just above the right temple and turn the palm obliquely upward. Look at the left hand. (Fig. 234 & 235)

Points to remember

(1) Coordinate the movements of the arms and the legs and complete the movements simultaneously.

(2) Coordinate pushing the palm forward with the bow step and the distance between the feet should not be too wide. Parallel the left hand with the left foot. Hold the torso in an erect and natural position.

21. Turning, Deflecting Downward, Parrying and Punching

图 236 **Fig 236**

(1) Turn the body and move the toes inward

Shift the weight rightward, sit back and shift the weight onto the right leg with the toes of the left foot turned inward. Turn the body to the right. Move both hands rightward, the right hand to the right side of the body and the left hand to the left side of the head, with the palms facing obliquely downward. Look at the right hand. (Fig. 236)

(2) 收脚握拳：上体继续右转，重心左移，左腿屈膝，右脚提收，右脚尖落在左脚内侧；右手逐渐握拳下落，经腹前向左划弧，停于左肋前，拳心向下，左手撑于左额前上方；眼看前方。(图 237、238)

图 237 Fig 237

图 238 Fig 238

(3) 摆步扳拳：右脚向前迈出，脚跟着地，脚尖外撇；右拳经胸前向前扳出，拳心向上，高与胸平，肘部微屈，左手经右前下落按于左胯旁，眼看右手。(图 239)

(4) 转体收拳：上体右转，右脚外撇，重心前移，左脚跟提起；右臂内旋，右拳向右划弧至体侧，拳心向下，右臂半屈，左臂外旋，左手经左侧向体前划弧，掌心斜向下；眼看前方。(图 240)

(2) Draw the foot and clench the fingers into a fist

Keep turning the torso to the right. Then shift the weight back onto the left leg. Bend the left knee, move the right foot and place the right toes on the floor next to the left foot. Move the right hand downward past the abdomen and leftward in an arc to the front of the left rib, with the fingers clenched into a fist and the knuckles turned up. Raise the left arm above the left temple. Look forward. (Fig.237 & 238)

(3) Step forward and punch with the fist

Step forward with the right foot, place the heel of the right foot on the floor and turn the toes outward. Move the right fist in a punch past the front of the chest forward with the knuckles turned down. Rest the fist at the level above the chest. Lower the left hand and press at the side of the left hip. Look at the right hand. (Fig.239)

(4) Turn the torso and draw the fist

Turn the torso to the right, move the right foot outward and shift the weight forward with the left heel off the floor. Rotate the right arm inward and arc the right fist rightward to the right side with the knuckles facing up and the right arm slightly bent. Rotate the left arm outward, the left hand past the side in an arc to the front with the palm turned obliquely downward. Look forward. (Fig.240)

图 239 **Fig** 239

图 240 **Fig** 240

(5) 上步拦掌：左脚向前上步，脚跟着地；左掌拦至体前，高与肩平，掌心向右，指尖斜向上，右拳翻转收至腰间，拳心向上；眼看左掌。（图 241）

(6) 弓步打拳：上体左转，重心前移，左腿屈弓，左脚踏实，右腿自然蹬直成左弓步；右拳向胸前打出，肘微屈，拳心向左，拳眼向上，左手微收，掌指附于右前臂内侧，掌心向右；眼看右拳。（图 242）

图 241 **Fig 241**

图 242 **Fig 242**

攻防含义

对方打来，用右扳拳格挡阻截，并旋臂右带；对方再打，我以左掌拦阻，以左手向右推开，以右拳直击对方。

练习要点

(1) 扳拦捶的转身动作要做到虚实清楚，转换轻灵，重心平稳。转换中要注意重心的移动、脚的扣转、腿的屈伸，切不可重心起伏，上体摇摆。

(2) 此势包含有扳拳、拦掌和打拳三个手法，多练习三个手法的规格，了解用途，再与下肢协调配合，正确掌握动作要领。

(5) Step forward and parry

Step forward with the left foot and place the heel on the floor. Parry with the left hand moving up to the front at shoulder level, the palm facing the right and the fingertips facing obliquely upward. Turn the right fist and draw it to the waist with the back of the right hand facing up. Look at the left hand. (Fig.241)

(6) Bow step and punch

Turn the torso to the left, shift the weight forward. Bend the left leg and place the left foot flat on the floor with the right leg naturally straightened to make a left bow step. Thrust the right fist forward in front of the chest and bend the elbow slightly with the back of the hand facing the right side. Pull the left hand slightly back and rest the fingers on the inner part of the right forearm with the palm facing the right. Look at the right fist. (Fig.242)

The meaning of attack and defence

When the opponent attacks, parry with your right fist and pull it rightward. When the opponent attacks again, protest yourself with your left palm and push him/her rightward with your left hand. Then hit him/her with your right fist.

Points to remember

(1) Keep balance while turning the body. When turning the body, remember to shift the weight, turn the foot inward and bend the knee. Avoid shifting the weight up and down or turning the torso right and left.

(2) Practise turning, parrying and punching and coordinate the movements of the hands and feet.

易犯错误

(1) 拦掌、收拳时两臂划弧过大,与转腰配合不协调。

(2) 重心起伏过大,身体歪斜,上下肢配合不协调。

22. 如封似闭

(1) 穿手翻掌:左手翻转手心向上,从右前臂下向前穿出,同时右拳变掌也翻转向上,两手交叉举于体前;眼看前方。(图 243)

(2) 后坐收引:重心后移,右腿屈坐,左脚尖翘起;两臂屈收,两手边分边后引,分至与肩同宽,收至胸前,掌心斜相对;眼看前方。(图 244、245)

图 243　Fig 243

图 244　Fig 244

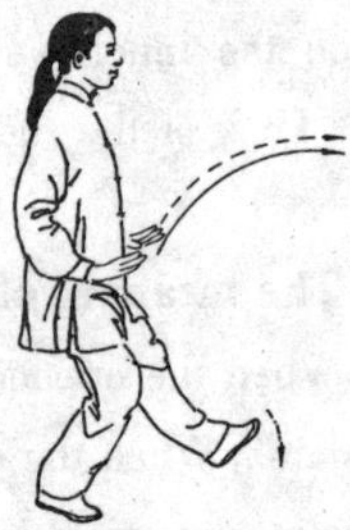

图 245　Fig 245

(3) 弓步按掌:重心前移,左腿屈弓,左脚踏实,成左弓步,右腿自然蹬直;两手翻转下落,经腹前向上向前推出,与肩同宽,腕与肩平,掌心向前,五指向上;眼看前方。(图 246)

Wrong movements

(1) When parrying and drawing the fist, the two arms draw an overwide arc and do not coordinate the movements with waist turning.

(2) While shifting the weight, move too much up and down and do not coordinate arm movements with legs movements.

22. Apparent Closing Up

(1) Cross the hands and turn the palms

Turn the left palm up and move forward below the right forearm and, at the same time, open the right fist and turn the palm upward. Cross the two hands in front of the body. Look forward. (Fig. 243)

(2) Sit back and draw up

Sit back with the right leg bent and the toes of the left foot raised, shifting the weight onto the right leg. Bend the arms, separate the hands at shoulder-width past the chest and pull them back slowly to the front of the abdomen with the palm facing obliquely to each other. Look forward. (Fig. 244 & 245)

(3) Bow step and press the palm

图 246 Fig 246

Shift the weight forward, bend the left leg and place the left foot flat on the floor to make a left bow step and the right leg straightened naturally. Press both hands forward with shoulder width. Keep the wrists at shoulder level and the palms face forward with the finger-tips upward. Look forward. (Fig. 246)

攻防含义

当对方用手推来时,我两手交叉插入其两臂之间,顺势引进,同时旋臂分开化解对方攻势,使其落空。当对方欲抽退摆脱时,我随即双手前按,乘势追击。

练习要点

(1) 后坐引手时,两手要屈肘旋臂后引,不可前上卷,两肘夹肘或抬高。

(2) 后坐时右膝屈坐不够,上体后仰向前挺髋。按掌时不要将身体向前俯身。

23. 十字手

(1) 转体扣脚:上体右转,重心右移,右腿屈坐,左脚尖内扣;右手向右分开摆至头前;眼看右手。(图 247)

(2) 撇脚分手:上体继续右转,右脚尖外撇,左腿自然蹬直,成右横档步;右手继续右摆至身体右侧,两臂平举于身体两侧,两腕同肩高,两掌心皆向外,指尖斜向上;眼看右手。(图 248)

图 247　　Fig 247

图 248　　Fig 248

The meaning of attack and defence

When the opponent pushes both hands against you, cross your hands and thrust them between the two arms of the opponent. Meanwhile rotate your arms to weaken his/her attack. When the opponent draws his/her arms, press them forward with your hands.

Points to remember

(1) When sitting back and drawing the hands, bend the elbows and rotate the arms as you pull the hands back. Do not press the elbows against the body or raise them high.

(2) Do not lean backward when sitting back. Keep the body erect when pressing the palms forward.

23. Cross Hands

(1) Turn the body and move the toes inward

Shift the weight onto the right leg. Turn the body to the right as the toes of the left foot turn inward. Move the right hand rightward to the front of the head. Look at the right hand. (Fig. 247)

(2) Turn the toes outward and part the hands

Keep turning the torso to the right. Meanwhile, turn the toes of the right foot slightly outward with the left leg naturally straightened. Keep moving the right hand rightward to the right side of the body. Move the arms to the sides with the wrists at shoulder level, the palms facing outward and the fingertips pointing obliquely upward. Look at the right hand. (Fig. 248)

(3) 扣脚搭手:上体左转,重心左移,左腿屈弓,右腿自然伸直,脚尖内扣;两手下落划弧,经腹前交叉搭手,右手在外,掌心向内。两臂撑圆,两腕交叉成斜向的十字,高与肩平;眼看两手。(图 249)

(4) 收脚合抱:上体转正,右脚提起向左收回半步,脚前掌落地,随之全脚踏实,两腿慢慢直立,体重平均放于两腿,两脚平行向前,与肩同宽,成开立步;两手交叉合抱于胸前;眼平视前方。(图 250、251)

图 249 Fig 249

图 250 Fig 250

图 251 Fig 251

练习要点

(1) 此势的手、腰转动和重心移动幅度比较大,同时配合两脚的扣转、外撇和收并。整个动作练习时要保持平稳、连贯、完整,中途不可停顿断劲。

(2) 收脚合抱时,不要低头、弯腰、突臀,两臂不要过紧。

易犯错误

第一、二、三个动作的脚不连贯,并两次移动重心。

(3) Turn the toes inward and rest one hand on the other

Shift the torso to the left and the weight slowly onto the left leg. Bend the left leg and naturally straighten the right leg with the toes of the right foot turned inward. Move both hands down in an arc and cross them in front of the abdomen, the right hand on the outside and the palms facing inward. Bend both elbow in a circle and cross the wrist obliquely above shoulder level. Look at both hands. (Fig. 249)

(4) Draw the foot and cross the hands

Bring the right foot half a step toward the left foot, place the front sole first and then the whole foot flat on the floor, straighten the two legs gradually and place the weight on both legs with the feet parallel and shoulder width apart. Cross the hands in front of the chest. Look forward. (Fig. 250 & 251)

Points to remember

(1) Coordinate the movements of the hands, waist and weight shifting with the movements of the feet. Keep all the movements smooth and without pauses.

(2) Do not lean forward and bow when drawing the foot and crossing the hands. Keep the arms in a comfortable position.

Wrong movements

The foot movements in (1), (2) and (3) are not smooth, and shift the weight twice.

24. 收势

（1）翻掌分手：两臂内旋，两臂翻转向下，左右分开，与肩同宽，举臂在胸前与肩同宽；眼平视前方。（图252）

（2）垂臂落手：两臂下按，两手落于大腿两侧；眼平视前方。（图253）

（3）并步还原：左脚轻轻提起与右脚并拢，脚前掌先着地，随之全脚踏实，恢复成预备姿势，眼平视前方。（图254）

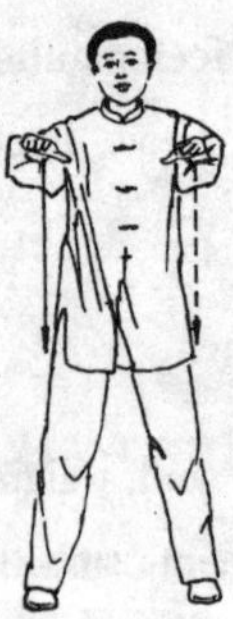

图252　**Fig 252**

图253　**Fig 253**

图254　**Fig 254**

练习要点

（1）翻掌分手时，要边分边翻转。

（2）并步还原时，左脚要注意“点起点落”，轻匀沉稳。

24. Closing Movement

(1) Turn the palms and separate the hands

Turn the arms inward and downward gradually and separate them shoulder wide. Keep the arms apart in front of the chest at shoulder level. Look forward. (Fig. 252)

(2) Lower the arms and hands

Lower both hands gradually to the sides of the thighs and the feet parallel shoulder wide. Look forward. (Fig. 253)

(3) Place the left foot next to the right foot and return to the original posture

Raise the left foot gradually and move it next to the right foot. Place the front sole of the left foot on the floor first and then the whole foot flat on the floor. And return to the original preparation posture. Look forward. (Fig. 254)

Points to remember

(1) Turn the palms as the hands are separated.

(2) Move the left foot slowly and gradually.

四、太极拳的技击要点

1. 太极拳推手

谈太极拳技击必先说说推手和懂劲,因为太极拳的技击和技击中的劲力是与其他拳种有很多不同的,所以能用太极拳功夫进行技击较量,并能在交手中取胜,没有推手训练和懂劲培养是不行的。

太极拳推手是把练拳者引入拳术技击的必要途径,只练拳架盘势不练推手,不可能领会到太极拳技击的真谛。推手又叫搭手、挤手、打手或擖手,以掤、捋、挤、按、采、挒、肘、靠等方法进行双人练习。

太极拳推手是在练拳架的基础上更进一步的功夫,是对抗性练习,与单练拳架有不同的效果,只练拳架而不练推手,很难深刻地领会太极拳的各种要求的内涵。当盘架子有了一定的功底后,可以通过推手培养"懂劲","懂劲"实际就是通过推手增强和提高人的感觉能力,灵活自如地运用拳架招法,逐步实现太极拳的技击效果。

通过推手练习,全身皮肤触觉和本体感觉的灵敏度提高了,对方的手或身体的某一部分接触自己的手或身体时,能立刻察觉对方劲力的来源去路、轻重虚实、长短、快慢,并及时沾粘,使其不能逃脱,巧妙地运用摩擦力的牵引作用,发挥"引进落空"、"乘势借力"、"以轻制重"、"以柔克刚"、"避实就虚"的技巧,牵动对方重心,成为我顺人背的形势,也就是使自己完全占居主动地位,在时间和力点上，寻找最为恰当的时机，运用力学原理，“以重制轻”，“以实破虚”地将全身劲力迅速集中于一点发劲攻击。

推手是获得太极拳技击功夫的重要手段，其本身也具有一定的技击实用性。虽然推手可以发挥技击效能，但它毕竟还不是实战，只不过是技击性练习，要达到太极拳真正的技击效果，“一触即发”，立决胜负，那是要在盘架子和推手的基础上学会了懂劲，越练越精，灵活应用太极拳技击方法，再通过技击性的“散手”训练，最终达到技击的目的。

2. 太极拳推手种类

太极拳推手练习的方式方法很多，常用的有下列几种：

(1) 单搭手法：两人相对而立，各以右(或左)脚前踏一步，用右(或左)手腕背侧相贴，往来推动。

(2) 单手平圆推手法：各以一手相搭，做水平环形推揉。

(3) 单手立圆推手法：各以一手相搭，做竖直方向的环形推揉。

(4) 单压推手法：两人搭手后做往来压腕动作。

(5) 双搭手法：右手及步法同单搭手法，但各以左手掌心扶住对方肘部，成四臂相搭，共成一圆形。

(6) 捋按推手法：两人推手时仅作捋按两个动作。

(7) 捋挤推手法：两人推手时仅作捋挤两个动作。

(8) 压腕按肘推手法：两人四臂相搭，作压腕按肘动作。

(9) 四正推手法：推手时练习掤、捋、挤、按四个动作。(又分原地和活步的两种。)

(10) 四隅推手法：(俗称大捋)推手时练习采、挒、肘、靠四个动作。从动作外形看起来好像都是捋的动作，所以又名大捋。

3. 太极拳推手要点

太极拳推手训练是培养技击能力的重要手段，更是培养懂劲的最佳方法，因此在推手时应遵循沾、粘、连、随的要点，个人的手臂和对方的手臂永远保持恰如其分的接触，不论动作怎样变化都不使手离开。

沾，是提高拔上的意思，凭个人推手技术利用对方反抗的力量，向上引起对方手臂，使其上体紧张，形成上重下轻，甚至使对方的足跟离地，目的是便于将对方发放出去。

粘，不论对方手法及身法如何变化，自己的手臂永远不离开对方的手臂，像把对方粘住似的。

连，推手中不与对方脱离，而且必须连绵接体，这就要使自己的力与对方的力有意识地连接起来，借以深入了解对方的力。

随，随着对方动作，缓急相随，进退相依，只要与对方搭上手，就不能使其逃脱，不论对方想怎样脱掉，自己的手都是要紧紧跟上去，这是借以取胜的机会。

沾、粘、连、随不仅仅是对两手的要求，身法、步法也是如此。不先不后，上下相随，周身协调一致。形要连，意要连，随对方的态势而伸缩进退，做到不丢、不顶、不抗、不离。对方进我退，对方退我进，对方浮我随，对方沉我松。用视觉观察，用身体感觉，探听对方力量的方向、大小等变化，并能引导对方形成背势，也就是使对方动作被动不得劲，不能灵活运转。当对方处于这种不利的形势时，发劲将对方发放出去，或用拿劲将对方拿住。

4. 太极拳推手中的劲力

通过太极拳推手的训练达到懂劲的目的，那么太极拳推手的劲力是什么样的？主要有哪些？下面谈一下劲力问题。

太极拳推手的劲力与力量是有区别的。力为有形，劲则无形，力方而劲圆，力涩而劲畅，力迟劲速，力散劲聚，力浮劲沉，力钝劲锐，这就是力与劲的区别。

先说说力。力有直力、横力、虚力、实力。直力显，横力隐，虚力刚，实力柔。力直而且虚这是真力，力横而且实这是劲。劲中分创劲、功劲、崩劲、粘劲等。创劲太直难以起落，功劲太死难以变化，崩劲太促难以斩接，这都是些强劲，且露形而不灵。功夫高深者多为粘巧劲，又灵又捷，又见其形，手到劲发。未击之前无劲，击中了仍无劲，只有在击中肯切之顷刻间，劲发疾如闪电，而且是一发便收，敛气凝神，毫不费力。

太极拳推手劲的种类繁多，不胜列举，但太极拳推手中尤以沾粘劲、听劲、懂劲、化劲等数劲为所擅长，也最具特点。

(1) 沾粘劲：即是推手中不丢劲，它主前进，是推手中最需要的基本内劲。这种劲训练到相当程度后，皮肤上好像有似云似雾的气，遇到敌手即如漆似胶粘搭不丢离。不但两手如此，周身也能如此。功夫愈高，气越厚，面积也越大。但是此气看不见，仅能自我感受，如有同样功夫者，则可互相感觉。因此，高功夫者与人推手，一搭手就知道对方的程度，其道理是在于彼此沾粘圆圈面积大小。

(2) 听劲："听"是指周身皮肤感觉的听，这只能在具备沾粘劲以后才能听，否则就不能听。

(3) 懂劲：能听，然后才能懂，如果听不准确，也就不能全懂。在推手中能闪、还、撩、转换、进退、行动自然、随心所欲，才可说是真懂劲。真正懂劲后，能得到屈伸动静的妙法，见入则开，遇出则合，看来则让，就去即升。如能达到开合升降的效果，到了这一层次的功夫，就可入神明之境域。

(4) 走劲：是不顶的劲，主后退，不懂劲就不能走，这里说的走是避对方的重力，不与其相抵。推手中一觉人有重力于我臂，马上变虚，遇偏重则偏松，遇双重则偏沉，泄去其力，随对方而去，不作抵抗，使人处处落空，毫不得力。走劲的枢纽在腰腿，腰腿无功，无从谈走劲。

(5) 化劲：化劲是由粘劲与走劲而成，不丢不顶，随感随化，前进后退，左顾右盼，相济不离。化劲在于我顺人背，能练出化劲，对方就是力大也无用。化劲中要略含掤劲，没有掤劲就不能化。化劲不只是手或肩用来化，重要在于腰腿。用手肩是硬拨，不是太极拳化劲，能顺从人之势以及劲路变化方向，随机应用，又不使对方知道自己的劲路，直到对方势背为止，这是真化。化后可拿可发，其中之奥妙是不化尽，化过了自己要势背，不能前进。化劲要等对方劲将出还没有全出、将到还未全到的时候，随势而化，不过早，不过迟，太早来劲未到，不能随势而化，过迟会被击中，化也无益。

(6) 引劲：引劲是对方不动，我引其劲，或对方动，我引其入自己的路线。引劲是处于化拿之间，较化劲更难。引劲是要引出对方背势中的焦点，引劲不仅是用手引，更需要身法、步法、腰法。引得越长，发时越有势。

(7) 拿劲：拿劲是发劲的前提，不能拿，就不能发。拿时动作轻灵，不使对方知觉，拿人要拿其关节，否则易被对方化脱。拿时注意沉肩坠肘，含胸拔背，敛气凝神，特别注意自己的重心稳定。

(8) 发劲：发劲是发放人的最后一击。发劲中又分截劲、长劲、沉劲、钻劲、寸劲、分劲、冷劲、抖跳劲等等。截劲较长，劲猛；钻劲较沉，劲厉；寸劲较分，劲狠；冷劲发人于不知不觉中，其势甚猛；抖跳劲是当自己的劲与对方的劲粘住时，利用腰腿的劲进行抖拍，就像拍皮球一样，使对方双脚离地腾起，被发出很远，高功夫者能先拍若干下，再以长劲发放，对方被发出后也能腾跳若干下，此劲非常奥妙。发劲的运用，必须把握机势、方向、时间。机势就是自己势顺，而对方势背，如对方重心已歪，身上某一部呆滞，要抓住这个时机发。方向是顺着对方背向而发，时间的掌握须是恰当其时，不可早，不可迟，早了敌势未完，容易发生顶抗，迟了会被对方发觉而生变化。发劲在距离上也有要求，远了劲达不到，近了自己的劲会被闷闭不能发。发劲在高低上下方面也有关系，那就是对方低我也低，对方高我也高，如对方过低我则发其上部，对方过高我则发其中部或下部。发劲时应求周身一致，意识果断，并且出于对方不知不觉中。

(9) 借劲：乘势借力，不早不迟，早了敌劲未出无法借，迟了自己会被击中。最恰当的时间是对方劲将出还没有出全，或将到而未到的时候，就在这一刹那借劲才能有效。

(10) 开劲：开劲是方劲，有开展的意思，用以攻入中门，其势勇猛，与身法、步法关系密切，距离也不能太远，远了用不上。开时须用腰腿劲，并意气配合。发力不只是手臂，以手臂硬开就会发呆发钝。开劲要与发劲配合使用，开到适当程度，也就是恰到好处，就应该立即转为发劲。开劲太过，易断，失去效用；开劲不足，反被对方所乘。开劲最佳程度，应该是开至自己顺对方背时为止。

(11) 合劲：是开劲的反面。有开就有合，合劲在太极拳中非常重要，发劲时多含此劲。如能将全身的气与劲力合而发其焦点，对方定受重创。

(12) 提劲：是拔高提上的劲，拔对方的根基使其重心倾斜，其势必败。提的巧法是乘对方不知不觉，往前进步，利用腰腿劲向上沾提。

(13) 长劲：伸长的劲。手臂、肘肩、腰胯、膝足或全身各部都可用、可发长劲。

(14) 钻劲：是一种入劲，拳掌出击如钻木旋转而入。

(15) 截劲：是一种刚劲，发出有直线和弧线两种形式，要随势应用。

5. 太极拳技击八法

太极拳把掤、捋、挤、按、采、挒、肘、靠八种最基本的技击手法，称为“太极八法”，它是太极拳所有拳式的基础，也是前述的太极拳劲力在运用中的具体体现，而每一法的运用又都需几种劲综合才能奏效。

本书在前面的章节对八法定义已有阐述，本节对八法运用的窍门及要点做一介绍。

(1) 掤，在于两臂要撑。

(2) 捋，在于掌中要轻。

(3) 挤，在于手背要横。

(4) 按，在于腰部要攻。

(5) 采，在于十指要实。

(6) 挒，在于劲力要惊。

(7) 肘，在于屈使要冲。

(8) 靠，在于肩胸要崩。

总的来说太极拳八法在应用技击中的劲力是经过长期训练实践练出来的一种灵活集中和运用自如的弹性力，要练成这种劲力，还应重视肌肉紧张和收缩的力量练习，而且应非常重视感觉灵敏和反应快速的神经训练，同时要十分强调运用正确的技术，合理地发挥肌肉的力量。松活缓慢的盘架子，应视为最基本的技术练习和导引气功的练习，它是为技击做准备的初步功法，不能与太极拳的实战技击混为一谈。

6. 太极拳技击要言

(1) 在瞬息有变的技击过程中，首先注意的是不失重。进退有法，落步有位，发手不过分，也不可够不上。过分和够不上，都是离开了重心点。要做到不偏、不倚、守中。如果偏前，那就是过了，容易被拉倒；偏后了就够不上，且容易被推倒；偏左偏右弊病相同。如果过分用大力推按，将完全失去重心，踉跄前扑，这就是倚的毛病。所以要立身中正，有支撑八面的势态和劲力。

(2) 太极拳技击手法高妙处在于不丢、不顶、不抗、不离。对手攻来我顺化其力，这叫引进落空。对方这招走空了要退，我随其退而发招发劲。这一发招，过早了就有了顶的毛病；晚了够不上，就是丢的毛病；根本不能引进，是抗的毛病；发劲不能奏效是离的毛病。

(3) 能刚能柔是太极拳技击本色，人刚我柔是太极拳特色。对方出力刚直，我接手如皮鞭物，紧紧缠搭其上，能放能展，使其不好摆脱；对方出大力，我搭粘其手腕，后坐身，并且化解其力，而后还击；对方来势急速，柔化则不能应付，必以截劲，不后不先，在其已发未到的时候，重击其肘关节或手腕手背，施以迎头痛击，这也是刚发的一种表现。

(4) 太极拳技击讲究后发制人，虽然是后发但要先至。对方不动我也不动，对方微动，我已动，这说的是精神注意警戒，对方要动的时候我已动之在先了。

(5) 太极拳技击讲究舍己从人，这也是说自己不先发动攻击，由着对方动，审时夺势，达到知己知彼，随机应变。能从人，才能得到引进落空的效果。

(6) 太极拳技击讲究不舍近求远，抓住机会发招为近，出手慌忙、上下寻机击敌为远。

(7) 太极拳技击讲究以静待动，心里要松净，外表要沉着冷静，静中又寓动，这样动起来全身才不会零碎乱动。

(8) 对方上部击来也要防下；进攻也要有后退的准备；正面不能进，可走偏门；左边被攻右边也须戒备；对方下盘稳固，可运用机智动摇其下部，其根基既动，对方就可被击倒。

(9) 取胜不在心，功夫越高，对敌时心里并不是很专注，也无需多少变化，即使身体受击也能随机化解其力，从容应敌，而击敌也只是在有意无意之间，这叫拳打两不知。

(10) 全部太极拳技击的精华奥妙处，可以说尽在虚实二字的运用。手、眼、身、法、步都有虚实变化，处处运用自如，那是需要有高深的功夫，才可能做到。

太极拳技击理论与方法博大精深，简言不尽，叙述不完，略谈梗概，仅供参考。

Ⅳ. The Essential Art of Attack and Defence in *Taijiquan*

1. Pushing-Hand in *Taijiquan*

Before getting into the art of attack and defense in *taijiquan*, let us discuss "pushing-hand" and "interpreting power", since the art of attack and defense in *taijiquan* and the force in the art of attack and defense are very different from those in other types of boxing. Therefore, without a good command of pushing-hand and interpreting power, it is impossible to attack or defend in *taijiquan*, let alone defeat opponents in combat.

Pushing-hand in *taijiquan* is the necessary access for the trainees to master the art of attack and defense in *taijiquan*. The essence of the art cannot be grasped until one practises both the boxing routines and the pushing-hand. Pushing-hand, also known as putting-over Hand, pressing-hand, striking-hand, or parrying-hand, is an exercise for two persons by means of warding off, squeezing, pressing, pushing, splitting, elbow striking, shoulder striking and rolling back.

Pushing-hand is a combat exercise, the purpose of which is different from boxing routines'. Without practising pushing-hand, one cannot deeply grasp the real intentions of *taijiquan*. After one has, to some extent, laid a solid foundation with the routines, he can train himself in interpreting power through pushing-hand. Interpreting power is a skill in the sensitivity and alertness gained through practising pushing-hand, with which one will use the boxing routines skillfully in order to achieve step by step the art of attack and defense in *taijiquan*.

Through the exercises of pushing-hand, one's skin's sense of touch and the body's sensitivity are improved so, when the opponent's hands or other parts of his/her body touch him, one will immediately be aware of it, find where the force comes from and where it goes, how long it will last, whether it is solid or weak, fast or slow, thus one can easily stick to the opponent, making the opponent unable to escape. Next, in order to have the opponent's weight under control, one should ingeniously use the drawing effort of friction and the skills of "making the opponent come to nothing", "seizing the opportunity and taking the advantage", "controlling heaviness with lightness", "utilizing softness to win over hardness", "staying clear of the opponent's main force and striking at his Achilles' heel", etc., so that the opponent cannot use his own force to resist. Thus, one will gain the initiative and put the opponent in a passive position. Finally, one may find an appropriate time and point to attack, applying the laws of mechanics and the skills of "defeating lightness with heaviness", "cracking emptiness with solidness", and immediately concentrate his overall strength on a point and attack.

Pushing-hand is a corner stone to learn the real skills of the art of attack and defense in *taijiquan* and is of practical use in combat. Pushing hand is more of an exercise for the art of attack and defense than a combat skill. To achieve *taijiquan's* real goal, i.e. to release one's own force and defeat the opponent, it requires interpreting power developed on the basis of boxing routines and pushing-hand. The more one practises, the more one will improve. The goal can be reached only by practising the basic movements of *taijiquan* and applying the essential techniques in the art of attack and defense.

2. Types of Pushing-Hand in *Taijiquan*

There are many ways to practise pushing-hand. The following methods are often used:

(1) Single hand on the opponent's hand

Two persons stand face to face. Then both take a step forward either with the left foot or the right foot. After that, put the back of the right or left wrist against that of the other's and push forward in turn.

(2) Single hand around a horizontal circle

Put one's palm against his/her opponent's palm. Then push around in a horizontal circle.

(3) Single hand around a vertical circle

Put one's palm against his/her opponent's palm. Then push around in a vertical circle.

(4) Press with Single Hand while Pushing

Place one's hand and the opponent's hand together and push forward, while at the same time bending the wrist

(5) Double hands on the opponent's

The steps and the movements of the right hand are the same as those is in "single hand on the opponent's". But both use their left palms to support the other's elbow, so that the four arms form a circle.

(6) Ward off and press while pushing hands

While pushing the other's hands, ward off and press them only.

(7) Ward off and push with efforts

While pushing the other's hands, only use warding-off and pushing hand with efforts.

(8) Bend the wrists, press the elbows while pushing hands

Both persons connect their arms, then bend their wrists, press the elbows while pushing hands.

(9) The Four Main Acts in Pushing-Hands

While practising pushing hands, one wards off, squeezes, pushes with efforts and presses. (Either with fixed stance or with moving stance.)

(10) Four additional acts in pushing-hands

(Popularly known as "big stroke")

While pushing hands, practise the four additional acts of splitting, rolling back, elbow stroking and shoulder stroking. It seems that all these movements are just types of stroking.

3. Essentials of Pushing-Hand in *Taijiquan*

The pushing-hand exercise in *taijiquan*, an important means to train the art of attack and defense, is the best method to develop the ability in interpreting power. Therefore, it is important to follow the essential points of adhering, sticking, connecting and following, and make sure to keep constant and proper contact with the opponent's limbs no matter how he/she changes his/her movements.

Adhering: Adhering means to lift and pull up an opponent. In order to defeat an opponent, one should, with the techniques of pushing-hand, take advantage of the opponent's force when he/she fights back and pull his/her limbs. Then his/her upper body will be tight, making his/her upper body heavy but lower body light. It can even make his/her heels leave the ground.

Sticking: No matter how an opponent changes his/her movements or routines, do not leave your arm from that of the opponent's, as if it is stuck to the opponent's arm.

Connecting: Do not separate from the opponent in pushing-hand. Keep it continuously attached to the opponent. It also requires one, with intentions, to connect his/her force with his/her opponent's, by which one can interpret the opponent's force.

Following: Follow the opponent's movement, no matter how slow or fast it is and no matter whether it is attacking or withdrawing. Once you touch an opponent, do not let him/her escape, even though he/she tries by every means. Follow him/her closely, as here lies your opportunity to win.

Adhering, sticking, connecting and following are not only the techniques for the hands, but also for the stance and steps. Follow the opponent closely and react to his/her actions at right moments. At the same time, coordinate with your entire body. Connect with not only the opponent's movements, but his mind as well. Then decide whether to attack or retreat accordingly. Remember not to lose, go against, resist, or leave the opponent. While he attacks, retreat; While he becomes solid, relax, and vice versa. Observe with your eyes, feel with your body, and notice the opponent's changes in direction of force and in strength. Do your best to make your opponent passive and unable to move or use his/her power. Then you can use your power to attack him/her, or just grasp him/her with your catching power.

4. The power in pushing-hand in *taijiquan*

The practice of pushing-hand in *taijiquan* aims at interpreting power. Let us now focus on what the power in pushing-hand is like and how it can be classified.

The force and power of pushing-hand are very different. The former is visible while the latter is not; the former is hard while the latter is soft; the former is indirect while the latter is direct; the former is slow, loose, floating and blunt while the latter is fast, solid, sinking and sharp. Such are the distinctions.

Let us first discuss the force. There are vertical and horizontal forces as well as empty and solid forces. The vertical force is apparent, while the horizontal force is hidden; the empty force is hard, while the solid force is soft. The vertical and empty forces are just forces, while the horizontal and solid forces ar powers. The power falls into the following categories: hurting power, fighting power, breaking power, sticking power, etc. The hurting power is too straight to rise and fall; the fighting power is too stiff to change; the breaking power is too fast to connect. Although these three powers are all strong, they can be easily discovered and rendered by an opponent. An advanced learner usually applies the invisible sticking power, which is effective and agile. The power lies wherever his/her hand goes. The power was not felt before or after a strike. Only when he/she hits his/her opponent's vital point, is the power felt, which is exerted with great swiftness and full concentration of the mind.

The different kinds of powers are too numerous to mention in *taijiquan* but the best and most distinguished ones are the sticking, listening, interpreting, neutralizing powers.

(1) Sticking power: With sticking power, there is no power loss while one is pushing his/her hand. It always advances and is the most necessary inner power. When one practises the power to a relatively high level, there seems to be some vital energy like cloud or fog on the skin not only of the hands, but also of the whole body, which sticks to the opponent like glue. The higher the level of techniques one masters, the thicker and wider the vital energy will be. But the vital energy can only be felt. It can not be seen. People with the same level of proficiency in *taijiquan* can feel each other's energy. That's why an

advanced learner can feel the opponent's proficiency in *taijiquan* as soon as he touches the opponent.

(2) Listening power: Listening means that the whole body "listens" to the force from outside. Without knowing the sticking power, one is not able to listen.

(3) Interpreting power: After one is able to listen to the power, it is then possible for one to interpret power. But if one is unable to listen properly, he cannot fully interprete it. Only when one has mastered all the movements in pushing-hand, such as flashing, attacking, knocking, changing, advancing and withdrawing, can he act naturally at his will. Only at this stage, can he acquire the ability to interprete power. Then he will have a magic power to bend, stretch, stop and move freely. When the opponent comes in, he opens; when the opponent goes, he closes; when the opponent advances, he retreats; when the opponent leaves, he follows. Once a person has achieved such results, he will have obtained a very high proficiency in *taijiquan* and will be able to concentrate his mind with little efforts.

(4) Neutralizing power: With neutralizing power, one does not hold out against the opponent's power, but to retreat. If one is unable to interprete power, it would be impossible for him to neutralize it, because neutralizing power refers to avoiding the strong force from an opponent and never going against it. For instance, one would change the arm to an empty one as soon as he feels a strong force coming from his opponent. The stronger the force is, the emptier one's arm should be, so as to try to deflate his opponent's "force balloon". He would never combat the opponent so that the opponent is unable to make use of his force to defeat. The waist and legs play a pivotal role in neutralizing power. If one has no power in the waist and legs, he will never obtain neutralizing power.

(5) Breaking power: The breaking power is the result of the sticking power and the neutralizing power. Do not retreat or fight against your opponent, but break his power when you feel it. Whether you advance or retreat, you should look back and forth. If one has a

good mastery of the breaking power and is in a favorable position, he can break the opponent's power no matter how strong its force is. The breaking power should contain some warding-off power, without which, the breaking power will not work. Breaking power is exerted not only with the hands and shoulders, but also with the legs in particular. With the hands and shoulders, one can only stir the opponent, but he cannot break the opponent's power. Real breaking power can be obtained only when one follows the opponent's movements, feel the opponent's change without making his own changes known, and make full use of his own advantage. After breaking the opponent's power, one can either catch him or release one's power. The important thing here is not to advance if you have not broken the opponent's power properly. Breaking power achieves its best effect when it is exerted at the point when the opponent is about to but has not fully released his power. Untimely exertion, either too late or too early, will lead to a defeat.

(6) Drawing power: With drawing power, when the opponent does not move, you make him move, or, when he moves, you make him follow your movement. The drawing power, which is more difficult than the breaking power, is between the breaking power and the catching power. Its purpose is to draw the opponent's vital point and throw him/her in an unfavorable position. Drawing power is exerted not only with the hands, but also with the step, waist and body. The longer one draws, the stronger one will be when one releases his power.

(7) Catching power: Catching power is a prerequisite to the releasing power. If one cannot catch the power, one cannot release it. In exerting the catching power, the movements should be light and agile, so that the opponent cannot detect the power. Catching power works best when it is exerted at the opponent's bone joints, otherwise, it will be easy for him to escape. When exerting catching power, it is important to sink the shoulders, drop the elbows, hold the chest in, straighten the back, hold the breath and concentrate the mind. It is also especially important to balance the centre of gravity.

(8) Releasing power: Releasing power is the last step in defeating one's opponent. It contains cutting power, distant power, sinking power, drilling power, short power, dividing power, cold power, shaking and jumping power, etc. The cutting power is harder than the distant power; the drilling power is sharper than the sinking power; the short power is firmer than the dividing power. One must release the cold power unconsciously but fiercely. Apply the shaking and jumping power when your power is sticking to the opponent's. Shake and strike the opponent with the power from the thighs and waist and, like bouncing a ball, bounce the opponent off the ground and, throw him a distance away. The masters can shake and strike several times, then release the distant power and hence bounce the opponent several times. The releasing power is profound and subtle so one should seize the right opportunity and exert it in the right direction at the right time. The right opportunity is when the situation is favorable to you but unfavorable to your opponent. For instance, when the weight of your opponent inclines or part of your opponent's body is stiff. The right direction of the releasing power should be opposite to the direction the opponent is moving in. Releasing power must be exerted at a proper time, neither too early nor too late. If you release your power too early, the opponent would still have power left to resist; if you release the power too late, the opponent would anticipate your intention and change his strategy accordingly. Furthermore, you have to pay attention to the distance between you and your opponent—when you are too far from your opponent, your power would not reach him; when you are too close to your opponent, your power would be blocked and therefore would not be released. Also important is the height of the releasing power. When the opponent's power is high your power must also be high, and, when the opponent's is low, yours must be lower too. But if the opponent's is too low, you can release your power at his upper body; if the opponent's power is too high, you can attack him at the middle or the lower part of his body. In general, you must coordinate the whole body, releasing the power without any hesitation and without letting the

opponent detect your intentions.

(9) Borrowing power: Seize an opportunity and borrow some power from the opponent. This action should also be undertaken neither too early nor too late. One cannot borrow the power from the opponent if one acts too early, and, one may be attacked if one acts too late. The most appropriate and effective moment to borrow power is when the opponent is about to attack.

(10) Opening power: Opening power means opening and stretching the power. It attacks the opponent's Achilles heel. This power requires close coordination with body movements and steps as well as an appropriate distance from the opponent. It will not work if one is too far away from the opponent. Be sure to use the power in the legs and waist and coordinate the mind with the energy. As it will be dull and blunt if one opens the power with stiff arms. Opening power should not be exerted only through the arms, but also through other parts of the body. Opening power should be combined with releasing power. When one opens the power to a certain degree, that is to say, properly, one should transform it into releasing power. Opening power is easy to break off if it goes too far, which means that it will have limited success. If one does not open the power enough, it may give the opponent a good opportunity in the fight. Opening power should be exerted to create a position favorable to oneself and unfavorable to the opponent.

(11) Closing power: Closing power is the opposite to opening power. Since there is opening power, there must be closing power. Closing power plays a very important role in *taijiquan*. When one releases power, he usually has closing power. If one can combine all his energy and force it into a focus to attack the opponent, the opponent will certainly be injured or incapacitated.

(12) Pulling power: Pulling power is the power to pull up. Pull the opponent's ground to make his weight incline. He then will be easily defeated. The skill of pulling is to make use of the power in the legs and waist and pull up when the opponent is not aware what is going on.

(13) Distant power: Distant power is a stretching power. Distant power can be released with the arms, elbows, shoulders, waist, hips, knees, feet and other parts of the body.

(14) Drilling power: Drilling power is a kind of penetrating power. One pushes his palm or fist into the opponent like a drill drilling into wood.

(15) Cutting power: Cutting power is a kind of hard power. This kind of power can be released in straight or curved lines depending on the situation

5. Eight Postures of the Art of Attack and Defense in *Taijiquan*

The "eight postures of *taijiquan*" refers to the eight cardinal postures of warding off, rolling back, pressing, pushing, splitting, pulling, elbowing-striking and shoulder-striking in the art of attack and defense in *taijiquan*. It is the foundation of all movements and detailed expressions of the power used in *taijiquan* which we have talked about before. But each posture is a result of the comprehensive application of many different powers.

We have discussed the definitions of the "eight postures", so in this session we will give a brief introduction to these postures.

1. Warding off —Using stretched arms.
2. Rolling back—Using light palms.
3. Pushing—Using horizontal backs of the hands.
4. Pressing—Using an attacking waist.
5. Pulling—Using solid fingers.
6. Splitting—Using impulsive force.
7. Elbow-striking—Using bent elbows.
8. Shoulder-striking—Using tight shoulders and chest.

Generally speaking, the power applied in the art of attack and defense can only be obtained through long-time practice. It is an agile and concentrated elastic power which can be freely used. To reach this level, one should pay attention to not only the training of external muscular force, but also the use of the mind. One must be sensitive and witty. Meanwhile, one should stress correct techniques and proper demonstrations of muscular force. Slow and soft movements should be regarded as the fundamental exercises of the techniques and the exercises leading to *qigong* are practice exercises for the art and should be clearly differentiated from attack and defense in real combat.

6. Essentials of the Art of Attack and Defense in *Taijiquan*

(1) During the fast changing process of attack and defense, the first important thing is to keep the balance. To do this, one must advance and retreat skillfully, make appropriate steps and do not stretch the arms too far or too near. If one should stretch the arms too far or too near, the body will move from its centre of gravity. One should not lean, but keep his balance. If one leans forward, he can easily be pulled down. When one leans backward, he would not be able to reach the opponent and is likely to be pushed over. It is the same when one leans too far left or too far right. If one goes too far when pushing or pressing, one will lose his balance and will stagger forward. This is a drawback of inclining. The body should be straight without inclining in any direction so as to withstand attack from all directions.

(2) The secret of the art of attack and defense is not to lose, resist, fight against or retreat. When the opponent strikes, you should neutralize his striking power by yielding and withdrawing. This is called "coming to nothing". When the opponent withdraws, you should stick to his body and release your power and attack him. You should not act too late or too early when you attack him. If you release the power too early, you would make a mistake of resisting. And if you release the power too late, you will leave the opponent's body.

(3) One characteristic of *taijiquan* is the coordination of softness with hardness. When the opponent is hard, you should be soft — opposition is the main characteristic of *taijiquan*. Therefore, When the opponent releases hard and straight power, your hands should, like whips, wind it tightly. You can prolong the "whip", so that your

opponent cannot get rid of it. When the opponent releases a lot of power, you should grasp and stick to his wrist, neutralize the power and then attack him. When the opponent's power is swift, you should not handle it with the soft neutralizing power, but break it with the cutting power at appropriate time, neither too early nor too late, fiercely attack his joints or wrists and the backs of his hands, and strike him soundly — an expression of releasing hard power.

(4) The art of attack and defense of *taijiquan* stresses overcoming the opponent's energy with the releasing power. Though you release your power later than your opponent does, the power should reach the opponent earlier. If the opponent does not move, you do not move. When the opponent moves even slightly, you should have already anticipated this and moved accordingly. That is to say, one's mind should always be sensitive and alert. When the opponent is about to move, you should have realized his intentions and should have already taken counter measures.

(5) The art of attack and defense of *taijiquan* also stresses giving up oneself and following the opponent. This means that you do not attack first but wait for the opponent to make a move while you observe the changing situation, get to know both yourself and you opponent, and take the initiative accordingly. Only by following the opponent, can you achieve the result of making the opponent "come to nothing".

(6) The art of attack and defense of *taijiquan* also stresses "never seeking from afar for what lies closely at hand". To seize the opportunity and release the power are those that "lie at hand", while to attack in a hurry and to look for an attacking point are those which are "afar".

(7) The art of attack and defense of *taijiquan* stresses remaining tranquil while waiting for the opponent's movement. One should stay calm with the mind relaxed and clear. But this calmness and relaxation is not idle by nature but is the kind of tranquility which embodies motion. Thus, the mind and body will work together harmoniously.

(8) When the opponent attacks the upper part of your body, you should not only defend the upper part but the lower part of your body as

well. When you advance, you should also be prepared for retreat. When you are not able to attack frontally, then try it from the side. When your left side is attacked, you should be alert on your right side as well. If your opponent's lower part is very firm and solid, think of a way to shake it. Once this firmness and solidity is shaken, he would then be easily knocked over.

(9) Victory does not lie in the mind. The higher one's level of technique, the less attention one pays to the opponent and to the basic movements. Even if one is struck, he would be able to neutralize the power with ease and attack the opponent just between consciousness and unconsciousness.

(10) The essence and secret of the whole art of attack and defense of *taijiquan* is the application of insubstantial and substantial power. The hands, eyes, body and steps can change between "substantialness" and "insubstantialness". Free application of these two kinds of power can only be achieved at a high level of mastery of *taijiquan*.

The theory and methods of the art of attack and defense of *taijiquan* are so broad and profound that they cannot be discussed exhaustively. This book is just a brief introduction and only for your reference.